Taming the ROTOZIP® Spiral

Projects and Accessories to Expand the Uses of the ROTOZIP® Spiral Saw

by **Joel N. Gessele**

by Joel N. Gessele

© 2001 by Joel N. Gessele.   All rights reserved

No part of this book may be reproduced, stored in a retrieval system, or transmitted by any means, electronic, mechanical, photocopying, recording, or otherwise, without written permission from the author.

ISBN 0-7596-7070-6

This book is printed on acid free paper.

Taming the ROTOZIP® Spiral Saw

About the Book

Plans and Directions for seven atypical projects and two accessories for the ROTOZIP® Spiral Saw.

Manual contains over 120 pages of project directions, illustrations, plans, and patterns. Directions include project sequence and descriptions of the results for the project. Projects and material recommendations permit efficient building of quality atypical projects using the ROTOZIP® Spiral Saw as the principal tool. Plans and patterns are available in an Appendix which supplements their presentation in the manual.

Triple the uses for your SCS01, SCS02, or RTM01 ROTOZIP® Spiral Saw.

Obtain directions, techniques, material lists, plans, patterns, and results on projects made using the ROTOZIP® Spiral Saw as the principal tool and apply the techniques to your projects. Many projects and techniques can be accomplished with conventional routers. Accessories can be modified to fit conventional routers. Review the illustrations and results to apply the experience to your projects.

Project plans and directions expand the techniques for using the ROTOZIP® Spiral Saw. Accessories permit standard router operations for dadoes and rabbets, portable rip fence, table routing, use as a panel saw, edge trimming, pattern routing, and case splitting. Techniques and accessories are illustrated to permit use of the methods on your projects. Instructions are included to save the craftsman's time by sequencing steps and suggest steps that improve the construction quality. Material recommendations and instructions allow construction of projects without lots of large tools or workspace.

Detailed directions and techniques emphasize the use of small set of common household tools to make the projects. Included are three sets of patterns and five sets of plans for the projects and accessories. Projects are Bull Wood Bank, Magazine or Scrapbook Box, Traditional or Modern sized cedar box trays to organize traditional cedar boxes or jewelry boxes, Cedar Bureau Box with tray rail, Electrical Box Covers, Bracket, Board, and Stringer Shelves, and. Computer Tables. Projects escalate in complexity to challenge an experienced woodworker, but detailed descriptions allow completion by the casual woodworker as projects are completed. The projects and accessories were selected to exploit qualities of the ROTOZIP® Spiral Saw and commercial materials. Projects were selected to utilize the ROTOZIP® Spiral Saw to solve construction problems
.

Project Name	Problem Resolved	Solution
Bull Wood Bank	Cutting matching parts without patterns or templates	Pattern routing and edge fortification
Magazine Box	Grooves and dadoes on delicate case parts	Expanded base to guide ROTOZIP
Bureau Box Tray	Small tray construction with common tools and equipment.	WorkBench to hold router
Bureau Box	Medium sized Jewelry/Document box made with common tools and inexpensive material.	Panel assembly, ripping, and edge trimming of medium sized cases.
Electrical Box Covers	Accurate guided cutting needed for presentable covers.	Covers made quickly and accurately without myriad of templates or patterns.
Bracket, Board, and Stringer Shelf	Construction of a strong, wide shelf without using premium materials	Stringers to position boards, portable groove routing and rabbeting.
Computer Tables	Large, strong case construction with Straw board and structural reinforcement.	Skeleton case members used to assemble large case.
Expanded Base	ROTOZIP depth gauge too unstable for routing and dadoing operations.	Expanded Base allows fence attachment and inverted use in WorkBench
WorkBench	Portable, storable, stable workbench needed for projects and speed setups for guided cuts.	Trash can used for base and work surface stablized with weights.

To encourage building of the projects , the projects employ a small set of tools that are usually available in most home workshops. I have limited the tools used to allow the casual woodworker to enjoy making these projects without a large outlay for tools. The procedures encourage the building of the projects where work and storage space is limited.

User built accessories are included to allow the hobbyist to build an inventory of accessories and templates.

Accessories are Expanded Base and portable WorkBench. Accessories can be self built to allow the ROTOZIP® Spiral Saw to be used as a panel saw, rip saw, and table mounted router.

Introduction

The inspiration for this manual has two sources, the desire to get the most from a small set of tools and to build useful projects quickly. Many projects require a large investment in tools to prepare materials for projects. If prepared materials could be used, the time and effort to produce projects could be reduced. Projects presented here use prepared materials to quickly build projects. In the interest of reducing tool and material costs, the tool accessories that are distributed with the tools are used or plans for the accessories are included. A limited set of common of tools is used so that the beginning hobbyist or the facilities challenged can make the items and the accessories.

The main tools used for these projects are ROTOZIP®, guidepoint bit, Sabrecut bit, drill, drill bits, select spade bits, select brad point bits, screw driver bits, screwdriver, framing square, and two 4" C-clamps. A WorkBench consisting of a garbage can and a square of plywood was used to make sure that these projects can be completed with a minimum of tools and equipment. A plan for a portable WorkBench is included to enhance its' capabilities and move the sawdust generation outside where cleanup is the rain or a wind storm. If you are facilities challenged, the WorkBench is easily stored, and the garbage can provides weather tight storage for materials and tools. The WorkBench was customized to aid in making the projects with greater precision and convenience.

Whenever possible, commodity materials have been evaluated and recommended. The evaluation and recommendation of materials that can be used without extensive preparation is necessary to make these projects viable with a limited number of tools and space to work. A comprehensive list of tools and materials for each project is included so that you can collect the materials to complete a project.

Detailed instructions are included to save time and relay the experience when the original project was rendered. An experienced user may only use the diagrams. A new user should find the instructions useful for preparing for a step and completing the step. The same experiences could be obtained by experimenting with scrap materials and not making an item. These projects do not preclude the use of scrap materials, but the effort may produce more than experience and sawdust.

Please review the ROTOZIP® operator's manual for recommendations on cutting direction, clockwise for freehand cuts, counter clockwise for guided guidepoint bit cuts. Cutting direction can determine the quality of the parts being cut. The portable fence and the fence clamped to the WorkBench give good results when used and even better results when the cutting operation pushes the project against the fence. Unmentioned in the operators manual are the suggestions for cutting when the ROTOZIP® is inverted and a fence is used. Most router project books provide addition instruction on cutting direction.

by Joel N. Gessele

Pay close attention to the manufacturer's recommendation to steady the ROTOZIP®'s depth gauge on the material to be cut. Bits are more likely to break if they are allowed to chatter when entering the stock or the ROTOZIP® is lifted from the material. When making plunge cuts, avoid the problem by using a tall fence and slide the locked depth gauge down the fence.

Three of the projects make intensive use of linear joints on tongue and groove cedar. An explanation of the terms is useful when using the instructions. A groove is similar to a dado. A groove follows the grain. A dado crosses the grain. A rabbet has only one shoulder and an open side. Stopped grooves and dadoes are recommended when unfilled joints would be seen if the joint was cut to the end of the stock.

Fig. I-01: Joint Definitions; Stopped grooves, Dadoes; dado cut for sanding (middle) completion, through Grooves, and dado for guidepoint edge trimming (right) completion.

ROTOZIP® Capabilities:

The ROTOZIP® is routinely displayed as a saw for construction and remodeling. Overlooked is its potential for some router applications. The ROTOZIP® was chosen because it has the potential to replace several tools. It is compact and can be used in place of several powered and hand tools. Its main features are the availability of inexpensive 1/8" bits and the 1/4" collet allowing the use of router bits. To get the most from your ROTOZIP®, the following projects and accessories have been assembled to show how the ROTOZIP® can be used for atypical projects.

In part, the projects are selected to exploit a capability of the ROTOZIP®, and afterwards to allow you to apply the experience on other projects. The Bull Wood Bank exploits the pattern following capability with the guidepoint bit and freehand cutting of small parts. The Magazine Box introduces the dado and rabbet joint for a simple sturdy open ended box. The Bureau Box tray exploits the flush trimming capabilities of the guidepoint bit and two case splitting operations with the Sabrecut bit. The Bureau Box is the first use of the WorkBench to cut square panels from 2 and 3 board panels and builds on the Bureau Box Tray experiences. The Electrical Box Covers use quickly prepared templates to make custom decorating accessories.

The greatest improvement that can be made to the ROTOZIP® is installing the circle cutter (part # CRCT1). It is the basic addition that permits the use of the ROTOZIP® when control and stability is needed. The circle cutter is invaluable for quickly making patterns and jigs to make straight smooth cuts that are not possible by manually guiding the ROTOZIP®. Buy it. Use it. It is a valuable inexpensive addition to the ROTOZIP®.

ROTOZIP® is a registered trademark of the ROTOZIP Tool Corporation.

by Joel N. Gessele

Tools used the in the Projects of: <u>**Taming the ROTOZIP® Spiral Saw**</u>

Project Name ---------- Tool	Bull Wood Bank	Magazine/Scrapbook Box	Cedar Box Trays	Cedar Bureau Box	Electrical Box Covers	Expanded Base	Portable Work Bench
ROTOZIP®+ Guide- point bit	Required	Required	Required	Required	Required	Required	Required
ROTOZIP® + Sabrecut Bit	Required	Required	Required	Required	Not Required	Optional	Optional
¼ " Straight cut bit	Required	Not Required	Not Required	Not Required	Not Required	Not Required	Not Required
1/8 " Straight cut Bit	Optional	Required	Not Required	Not Required	Not Required	Not Required	Not Required
Decorative router bits	Not Required	Not Required	Not Required	Not Required	Required	Not Required	Not Required
Framing Square	Required	Required	Required	Required	Not Required	Optional	Required
Drill + 1/8" bit	Required	Not Required	Not Required	Not Required	Required	Required	Required
!/8 " Brad Point Bit	Required	Not Required	Not Required	Not Required	Not Required	Required	Not Required
¼ " Drill bit set	Required	Not Required	Not Required	Not Required	Not Required	Optional	Required
Work- Bench	Optional	Optional	Required	Required	Optional	Optional	Optional
Expanded Base and Circle Cutter	Not Required	Required	Required	Required	Not Required	Not Required	Optional
6" Rasp	Required	Required	Required	Required	Required	Required	Required
Spade Bits	Required	Not Required	Not Required	Not Required	Not Required	Not Required	Not Required
Belt Sander	Optional	Not Required	Not Required	Not Required	Not Required	Not Required	Not Required
Pad Sander	Optional	Optional	Optional	Optional	Optional	Optional	Optional
4"C- Clamps	Required	Required	Required	Required	Required	Required	Required
Screw driver/bit	Required	Not Required	Not Required	Not Required	Required	Required	Required
Wood Chisel	Optional	Optional	Optional	Required	Optional	Optional	Optional
Hand Saw	Optional	Optional	Optional	Required	Optional	Optional	Optional

Legend:	Required	Optional	Not Required

Taming the ROTOZIP® Spiral Saw

Projects 4
Bull Wood Bank 6
   Bull Wood Bank : Description: 6
   Bull Wood Bank : Materials 7
   Bull Wood Bank : Tools 7
   Bull Wood Bank : Plan 8
   Bull Wood Bank : Blueprint 8
   Bull Wood Bank : Cutting 8
   Bull Wood Bank : Preparation for Assembly 19
   Bull Wood Bank : Assembly 20
   Bull Wood Bank : Finish 22
   Bull Wood Bank : Results 22
Magazine Box or Scrap Book Holder: 24
   Magazine Box or Scrap Book Holder: Description 24
   Magazine box: Materials 25
   Magazine box: Tools 25
   Magazine box: Plan 26
   Magazine box: Blueprint 26
   Magazine Box: Cutting 27
   Magazine box: Preparation for Assembly 28
   Magazine box: Assembly 28
   Magazine box: Finish 29
   Magazine box: Results 29
Bureau Box Tray : 31
   Bureau Box Tray: Description 31
      Traditional: 32
      Modern 32
   Bureau Box Tray: Tools 32
   Bureau Box Tray: Blueprint 33
   Bureau Box Tray: Cutting 35
   Bureau Box Tray: Preparation for Assembly 35
   Bureau Box Tray: Assembly 37
   Bureau Box Tray: Finish 43
   Bureau Box Tray: Results 43
Bureau Box: 46
   Bureau Box: Description 46
   Bureau Box: Materials 49
   Bureau Box: Tools 50
   Bureau Box: Plan 50
   Bureau Box: Blueprint 51
   Bureau Box: Cutting 52
   Bureau Box: Assembly 55
   Bureau Box: Finish 58
   Bureau Box: Results 59
Electrical box cover: 66

Electrical box cover: Description 66
Electrical Box cover: Materials: 67
Electrical Box cover: Tools 67
Electrical box cover: Plan 67
Electrical box cover: Blueprint 67
Electrical box cover: Cutting 67
Electrical box cover: Preparation for Assembly 71
Electrical box cover: Assembly 71
Electrical box cover: Finish 71
Electircal Box cover: Results: 71
Bracket, Board and Stringer shelf: 73
Bracket, Board and Stringer shelf: Description 73
Bracket, Board and Stringer shelf: Materials 76
Bracket, Board and Stringer shelf: Tools 76
Bracket, Board and Stringer shelf: Plan 76
Bracket, Board and Stringer shelf: Blueprint 77
Bracket, Board and Stringer shelf: Cutting 77
Bracket, Board and Stringer shelf: Preparation for Assembly 80
Bracket, Board and Stringer shelf: Assembly 80
Bracket, Board and Stringer shelf: Finish 82
Bracket, Board and Stringer shelf: Results 82
Computer Table: 86
Computer Table: Description 86
Computer Table: Materials 88
Computer Table: Tools 89
Computer Table: Plan 89
Computer Table: Blueprint 90
Computer Table: Cutting 93
Computer Table: Preparation for Assembly 95
Computer Table: Assembly 98
Computer Table: Finish 99
Computer Table: Results 100
Appendix 103
Expanded Base: 103
Expanded Base: Cutting directions 105
Expanded Base: Ripping 108
Expanded Base: Stopped Dadoes 109
Speed or Framing square: 110
Setup Spacer 110
WorkBench 110
WorkBench: Materials 112
WorkBench: Tools 113
WorkBench: Accessories 113
WorkBench: Blueprint 113
WorkBench: Frame 113

WorkBench: Expanded Base 114
WorkBench: Weighting 114
WorkBench: Clamp 115
WorkBench: Fence 115
WorkBench: Guidepoint Flush Trimming 116
Directory of Plans and Patterns 124

by Joel N. Gessele

Projects

by Joel N. Gessele
Bull Wood Bank

Fig. 1-01: Assembled, sanded, Short Horn Bull and Shellac Finished Long Horn Bull with felt eyes and tongue.

Bull Wood Bank   : Description:

The Bull Wood Bank emphasizes the use of the guidepoint bit to make similar parts. The Bull Wood Bank was selected because it exploits the capabilities of the ROTOZIP® in copying parts. This combined with the ROTOZIP®'s ability to produce a smooth edge reduces the effort to complete a finished bank. The ROTOZIP® reduces the need to sand, cut pilot holes, and stop to thread a jig saw blades. Originally I tried to avoid tracing the outlines on each piece. However, the outline provides a useful reference even when a pattern is being followed. The cutting directions are written to cut project pieces in a single thickness without having to trace patterns on all the stock. This approach was chosen to reduce the load on the ROTOZIP® and give experience in cutting parts from patterns. Cutting the bank from single thicknesses is useful as an alternative to high capacity band saw and still not exceed the one inch the capacity of the ROTOZIP®.

Premium materials for this project are hardwoods, but plywood and OSB are acceptable for projects that will be painted. Using the material that you will be cutting most frequently is preferred to give experience with the material and ROTOZIP®, however I think that a drywall bank would be heavy and the horns fragile.

Taming the ROTOZIP® Spiral Saw

The 1/8 " dowels were added to aid in assembly. An alternative to slow drying glues is to use contact cement and the dowels can be used selectively to assist in aligning parts. Either way this method will lead to a Bank that will really hold a nose full of nickels.

The cutting directions are an aid in constructing the Bull Wood Bank Eight parts comprise the bank. The steps of the directions have been added to the overview of the parts. The parts are named and displayed in their final assembled sequence.

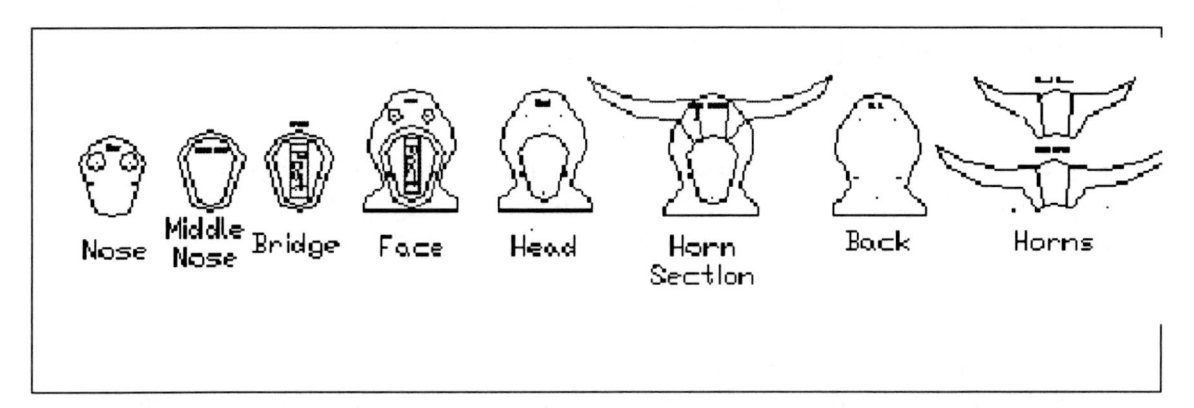

Fig. 1-02: Bull Wood Parts overview and Part Names as used in Cutting directions. Blue text designate labels or assembly aids.

The Nose and Back are solid parts. The Middle Nose, Bridge, Face, Head, and Horn Section have a coin cavity. Two Horn patterns were tried. The Long Horn is too large for regular paper and is presented as a half pattern.

Cutting parts with a pattern underneath is faster and produces parts that are uniform. The direction is counterclockwise. The effort to smooth the edge and fortify the edge to cut the next part does not add significantly to the work that wouldn't be done in the normal course of producing the parts. The cutting of parts with patterns underneath yields a varied experience. Some pieces cut with difficulty, others so easy that I didn't believe I was following the pattern. Critical to the pattern assisted cutting is positioning the guidepoint bit correctly. If the bit is too high or low, it mars the pattern or feels like the bit is dull. The best results are achieved when the cutting proceeds continuously and smoothly, minimizing the burnishing of the pattern.

Bull Wood Bank : Materials:

1 — Approximately 6 feet of 5 ½ " wide ¾ " thick stock.
2 — 1 inch wood or drywall screws (for holding parts to post and parts and patterns to WorkBench)
2 — ¾ " inch wood or drywall screws (for holding Post to WorkBench)
   Wood Glue and Saw Dust (make paste to fill irregularities)
    Crazy Glue (for fortifying pattern surfaces and dowel holes)

Bull Wood Bank : Tools

by Joel N. Gessele

Drill, 1/8" bit (dowel holes).
¾ " and ½ " forstner or spade bit (eyes and nostrils)
Screwdriver or screwdriver bit for drill
1/8 " dowel
6" wood rasp
Wood chisel (optional, could use rasp as alternate)
Round over router bit (optional, could use rasp as alternate)
Belt sander (optional, could use rasp as alternate)
Sandpaper or sanding pad

Bull Wood Bank : Plan

See Fig. 1-1 for overview of the Wood Bull parts. The patterns for tracing or cutting are in the Appendix. The method that evolved is covered in the Cutting Directions. If 6" (5 1/2" planed) stock is used, grain will be vertical for the Face and Back, vertical grain in the Nose is also desired.

Bull Wood Bank : Blueprint

See Appendix for patterns. Patterns included are: Face, Head, Horn Section, Back, Bridge, Middle Nose, Nose and Horn patterns. Excellent results can be obtained by piercing the dowel hole centers with pins, cutting the outline of the stacked (Head) patterns for placement on the stock with Spray adhesive. Full size patterns are needed because the parts are complex and accuracy is needed in cutting and assembly.

Bull Wood Bank : Cutting

1. Set the guidepoint bit in collet for cutting ¾ " material and adjust the depth gauge. According to manufacture's directions the bit should extend an ¼ " below the stock to be cut.

2. Transfer the Face pattern to ¾ " stock and mount to a 1 x 2 x 3 post (see Work bench suggestions in Appendix) on the WorkBench or a board that can be clamped to a solid work surface using 1 " wood screws.

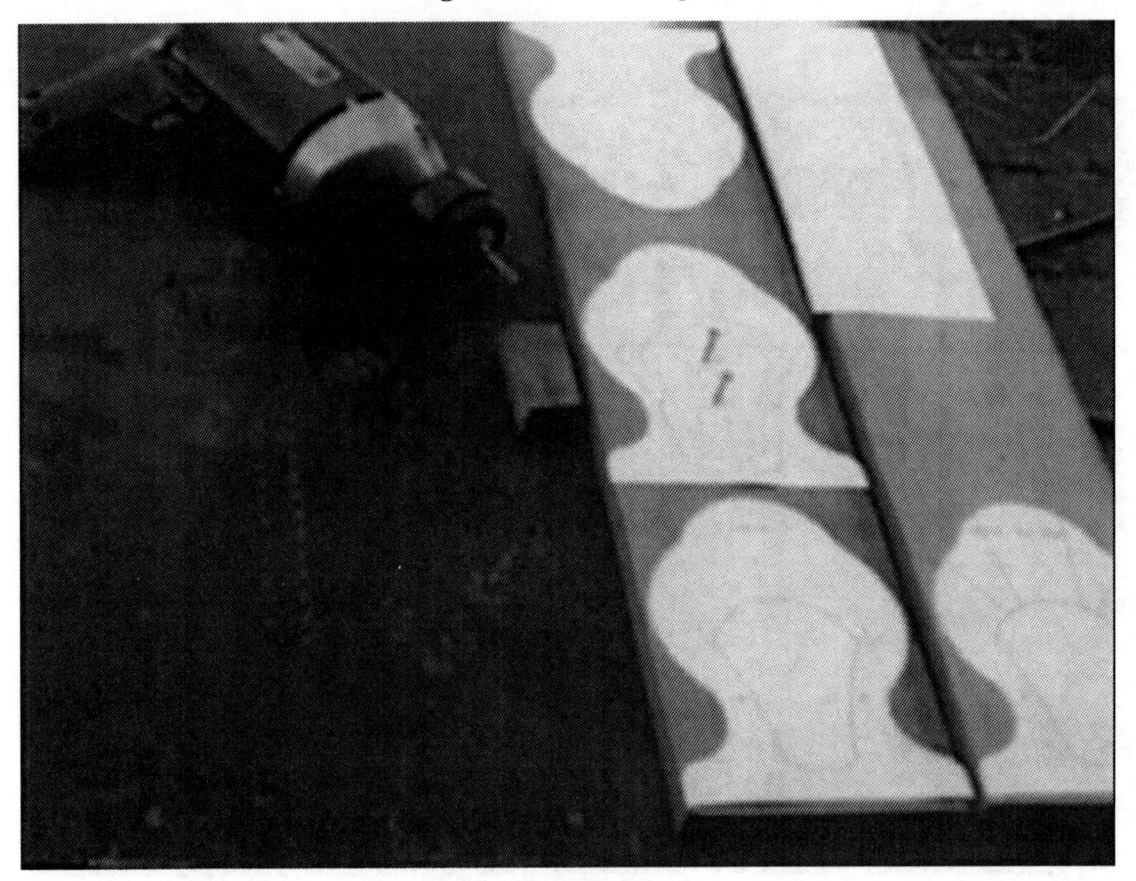

Fig. 1-03: Setup for cutting Face from 6 inch boards: Post, Board 1: Head, Face (with Screws started for fastening to Post), Back; Board 2: Horn section and Short Horn patterns on Stock. Electric drill points to Post. The post serves two functions, a place to hold the stock and a spacer to elevate the stock above the surface for the Spiral saw bit. In this case, the pattern was attached to the stock with Spray Adhesive to provide a pattern for freehand cutting the Face.

3. Cut outline, then cut inner coin cavity,

by Joel N. Gessele

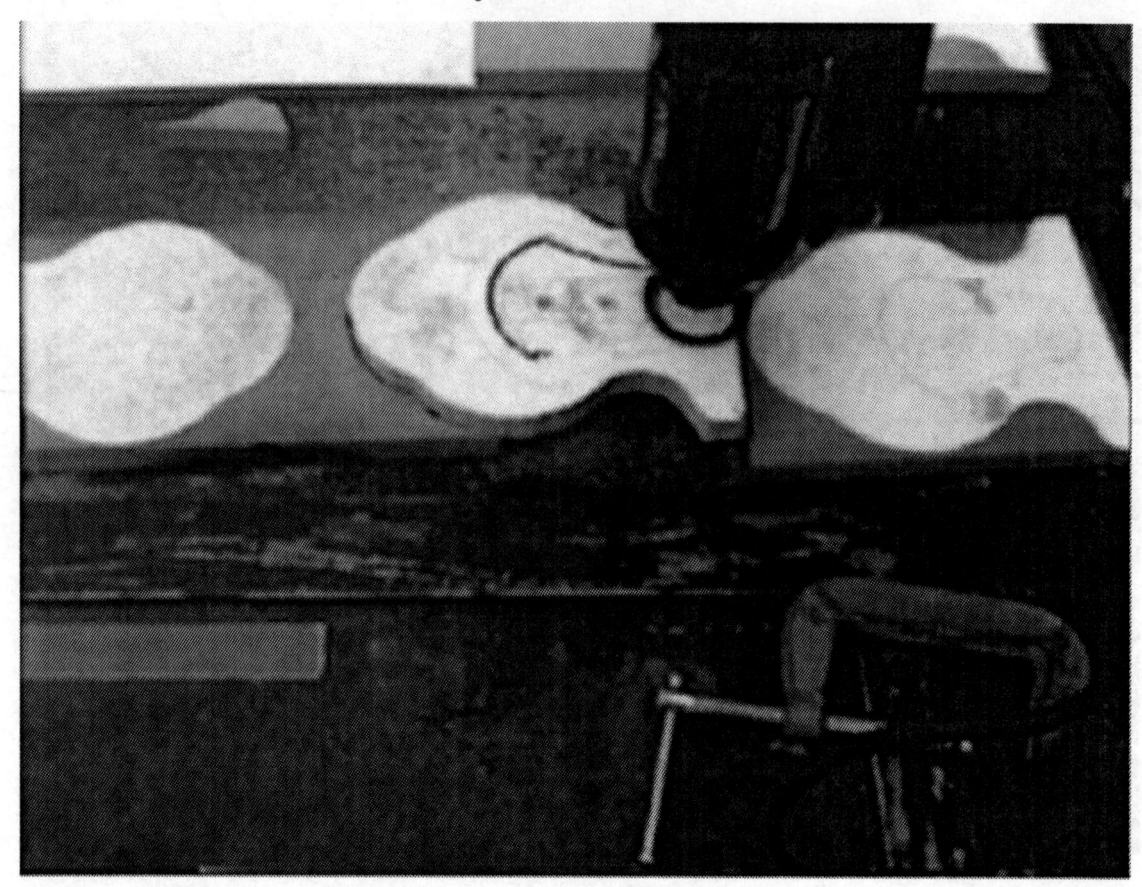

Fig. 1-04: Outline cut complete, Coin cavity cut 2/3 complete. Straight cut at bottom used framing square clamped with C-clamps to guide Spiral Saw. The direction of the freehand cut is clockwise. Two other parts will be cut from the board. The two other parts are set in their original orientations to the Face. 4. Fill irregularities that may have resulted during the cutting, set aside to allow filler to dry. (Start Step 5) Smooth edges of outline and coin cavity with rasp.

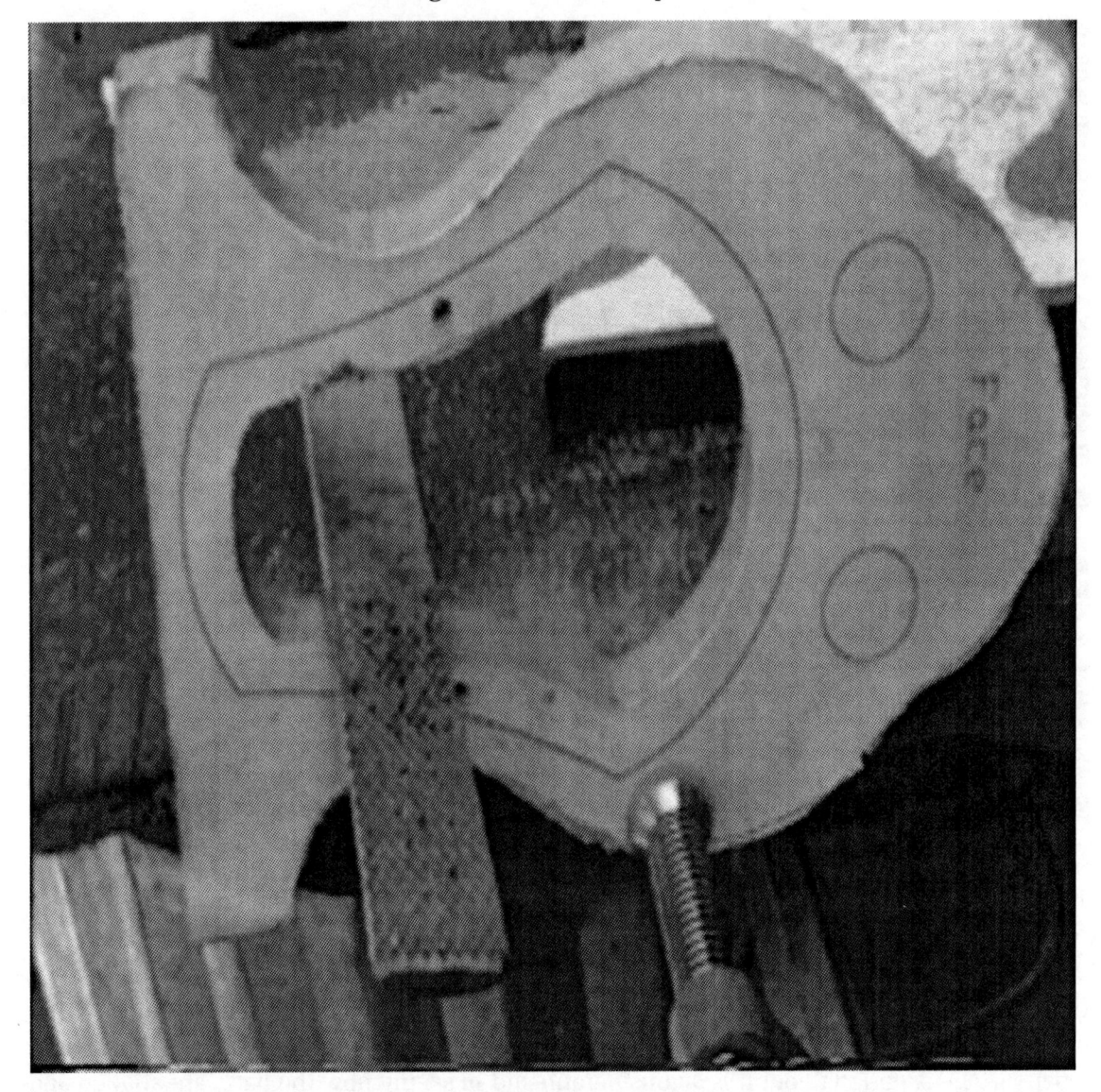

Fig. 1-05: Outline edges and coin cavity edges of the Face prepared as pattern to guide cutting of Head section. Fortify trailing edges of Face with Crazy Glue.

5. Transfer the Head pattern to ¾ " stock and attach the head stock to the work bench with the Face underneath to serve as the pattern for the Head. As you gain experience, putting the pattern on the stock may not be necessary. It is recommended at this point to aid in cutting parts with a pattern underneath.

by Joel N. Gessele

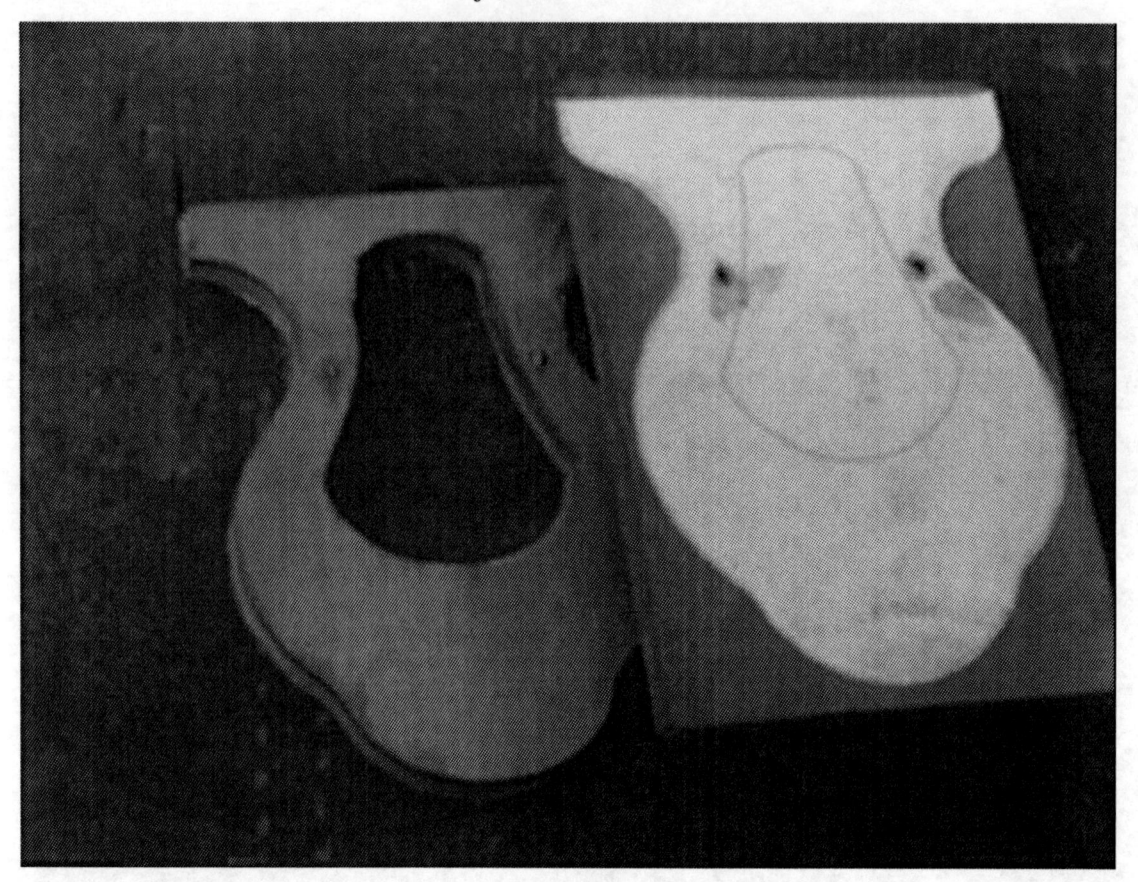

Fig. 1-07: Face part secured to benchtop with screws protruding to aid in positioning the Head for pattern assisted cutting. Pronounced holes in Head pattern indicate application of Crazy Glue to fortify dowel holes that are being used to position the Head in relation to the Face dowel holes. Screws show through the Face to position the Head and hold it in place for cutting using the Face as a pattern underneath. Direction of the cut is counterclockwise, the guidepoint bit uses the Face as a pattern. Cut the outline and the coin cavity. Pattern on upper surface is optional, but it is a considerable aid in seeing how the parts are aligned and viewing the progress of the cut. Both cuts are counter clockwise, allowing the cutting action to pull the bit to the edge of the Face pattern underneath.

6. Remove the screws holding the completed parts to the WorkBench. Fill irregularities that may have resulted during the cutting, set aside to allow filler to dry. Smooth edges of outline and coin cavity with rasp. Fortify trailing edges of Head with Crazy Glue.

7. Apply the Horn Section pattern to ¾ " stock, drill and fortify the dowel holes. Attach the Horn section to the work bench with the prepared Head section underneath as the pattern and spacer. Use 1" long screws from the bottom of the plywood square at the dowel holes.

8. Cut the outline and the coin cavity using the Head underneath to assist in guiding the ROTOZIP® guidepoint bit.

Taming the ROTOZIP® Spiral Saw

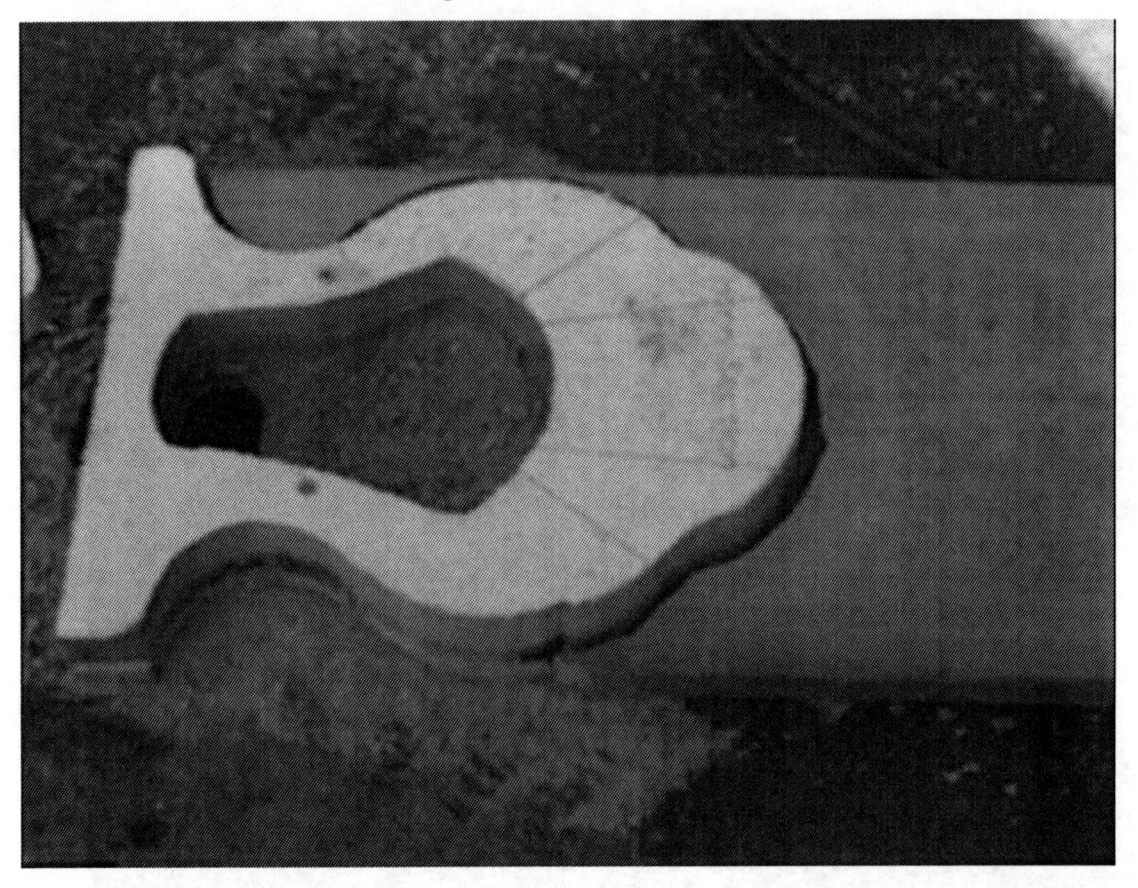

Fig. 1-08: Horn Section cut completed. Head section is underneath. Rays on pattern are the edges of the Horns, outer rays indicate cutting lines for fitting Horns inner rays are from the Horns, where the coin slot will be cut in the Horns. If you're really short on material, the material between the outer rays can be omitted.

9. Fill irregularities that may have resulted during the cutting, set aside to allow filler to dry. Smooth edges of outline and coin cavity with rasp. Fortify outer trailing edges of Horn Section with Crazy Glue. A considerable section of the Horn section will be removed when the Horns are fitted. Including this section on the part will allow you to adjust the fit of the horns and cut the Back.

10. Transfer the Back pattern to the stock, secure stock and Horn Section to the plywood square from underneath using the 1" screws at the dowel Hole positions. The dowel holes are only started in the stock for the Back not drilled through where they would be seen. The holes are fortified with Crazy Glue.

11. Cut the outline and the coin cavity using the Horn Section underneath to assist in guiding the ROTOZIP®.

by Joel N. Gessele

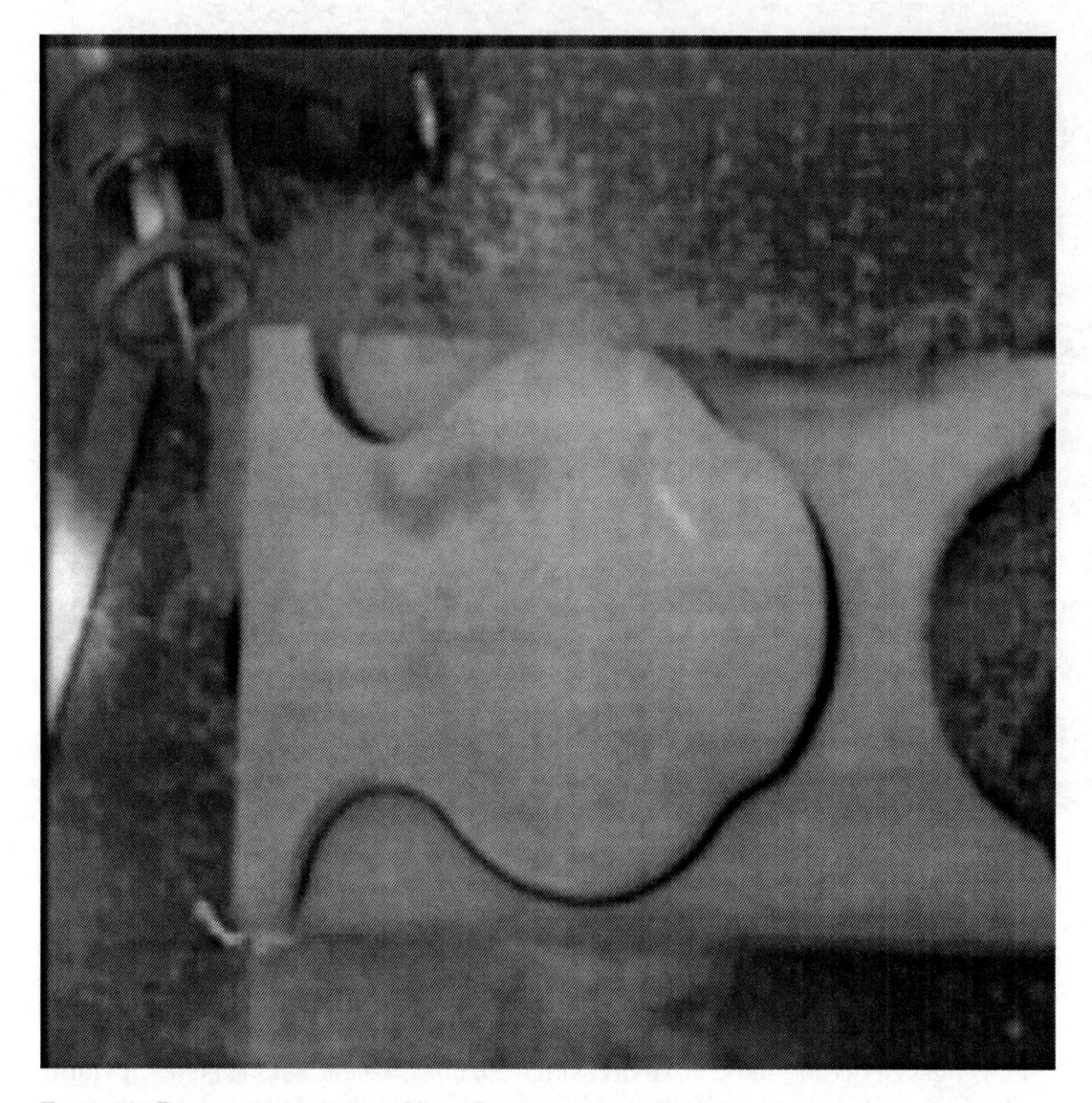

Fig 1-09: Back cut completed. Horn Section underneath served as pattern, screws pass through Horn section and part of way into Back. Back pattern is facing down because dowel holes were drilled through the pattern (Horn Section) but not the Back stock.

12. Transfer the Bridge pattern to the stock. Prepare the Bridge for mounting on the Post for freehand cutting. The Bridge and Middle nose pieces are only 3/8 " wide, be sure to drill the dowel holes and fortify the holes before cutting the outline or the coin cavity.

13. Mount the Bridge part on the post and cut the outline and the coin cavity, releasing the Bridge part from the Post.

Taming the ROTOZIP® Spiral Saw

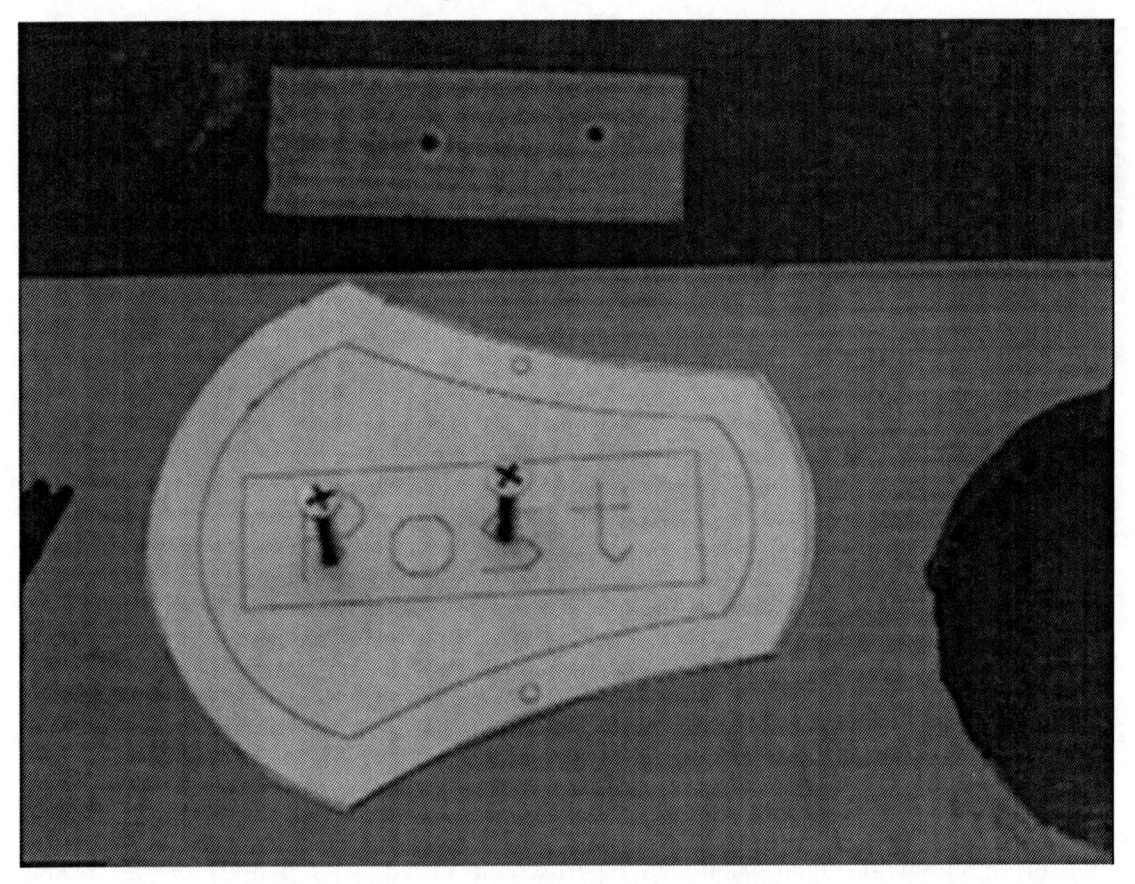

Fig. 1-10: Post and Bridge stock with screws started in Bridge ready for mounting on Post. The pattern included marks for the screws to hold it to the post. Pre-drilled holes will avoid cracking the post when the Bridge is attached. Post is in the background, attached to the plywood square with screws through the plywood

Fill irregularities, smooth external and internal surfaces with the surfaces and fortify the surfaces with Crazy Glue.

14. Transfer the Middle nose pattern to the stock, drill and fortify the dowel holes, secure stock and Bridge to the plywood square from underneath using the 1" screws at the dowel hole positions.

15. Cut the outline and the coin cavity using the Bridge underneath to assist in guiding the ROTOZIP®. Both the outline and the coin cavity cuts are counter clockwise cuts because the pattern is beneath the Middle Nose part.

by Joel N. Gessele

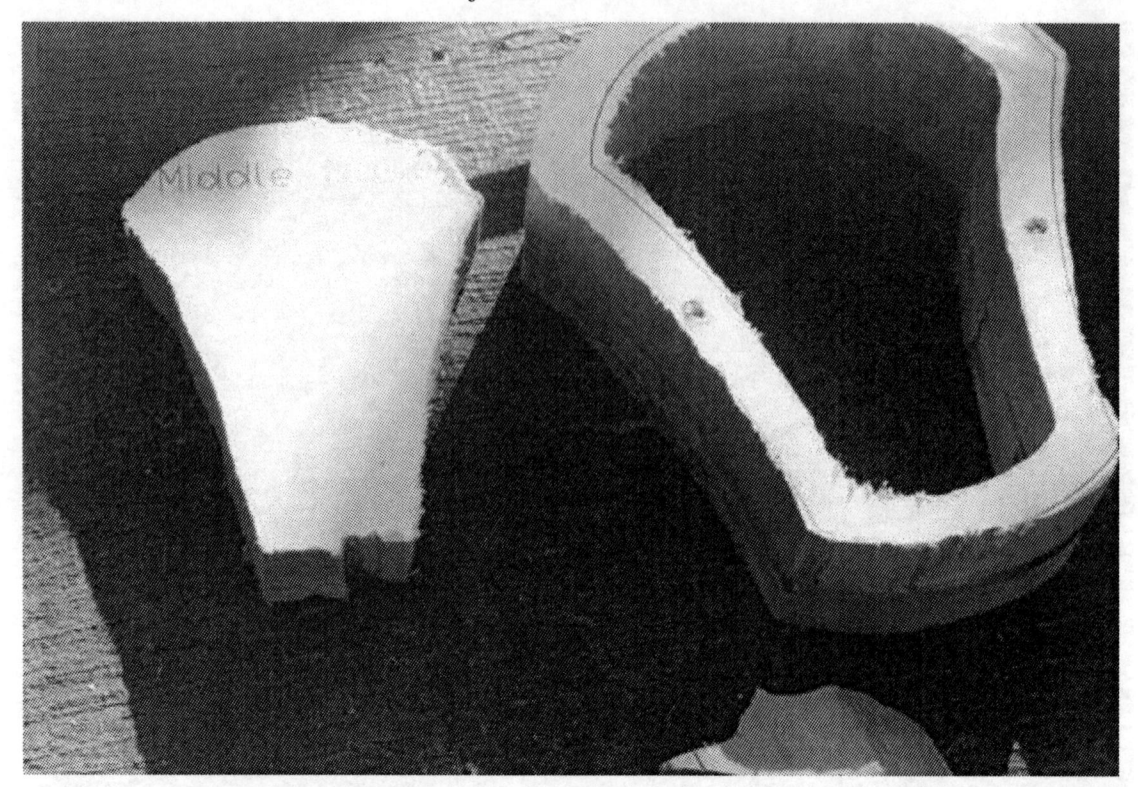

Fig. 1-11: Middle Nose cut completed, Coin cavity removed, Middle nose held in place by screws through plywood square, and bridge part which served as the pattern for the Middle Nose.

16. Fill irregularities on the outer surface that may have resulted during the cutting, smooth the edges with the rasp, and fortify the edge with Crazy Glue.

17. Transfer the Nose pattern to stock, drill the dowel hole part way into the Nose stock.

18. Mount the Nose with the Middle Nose part underneath to be the pattern for the outline cut. Cut the nose.

19. Draw the Horn Pattern on ½ " stock that matches the thickness of the Coin Slot section. The Horns and the Horn Section can be seen in Fig. 1-03 as Board 2. Cut the outline freehand.

20. Fortify the Horn tips and coin slot ends. Smooth the Horns and begin fitting the Horns to the Horn section. Complete the smoothing of the outline of the Horns, including the lower part that will replace the section between the rays of the Horn section. The completed Horns will determine the section to be removed from the Horn Section.

21. Clamp the Horns to a flat surface with sufficient clearance for the ROTOZIP® depth gauge from the coin slot rays. Install a ¼ " straight cutting bit with the ¼ " collet and adjust

Taming the ROTOZIP® Spiral Saw

the depth to 1/8 ". Cut three dadoes, 1/8 " deep to guide the forming of the coin slot. Remove the material between the dadoes with a wood chisel and finish with the rasp.

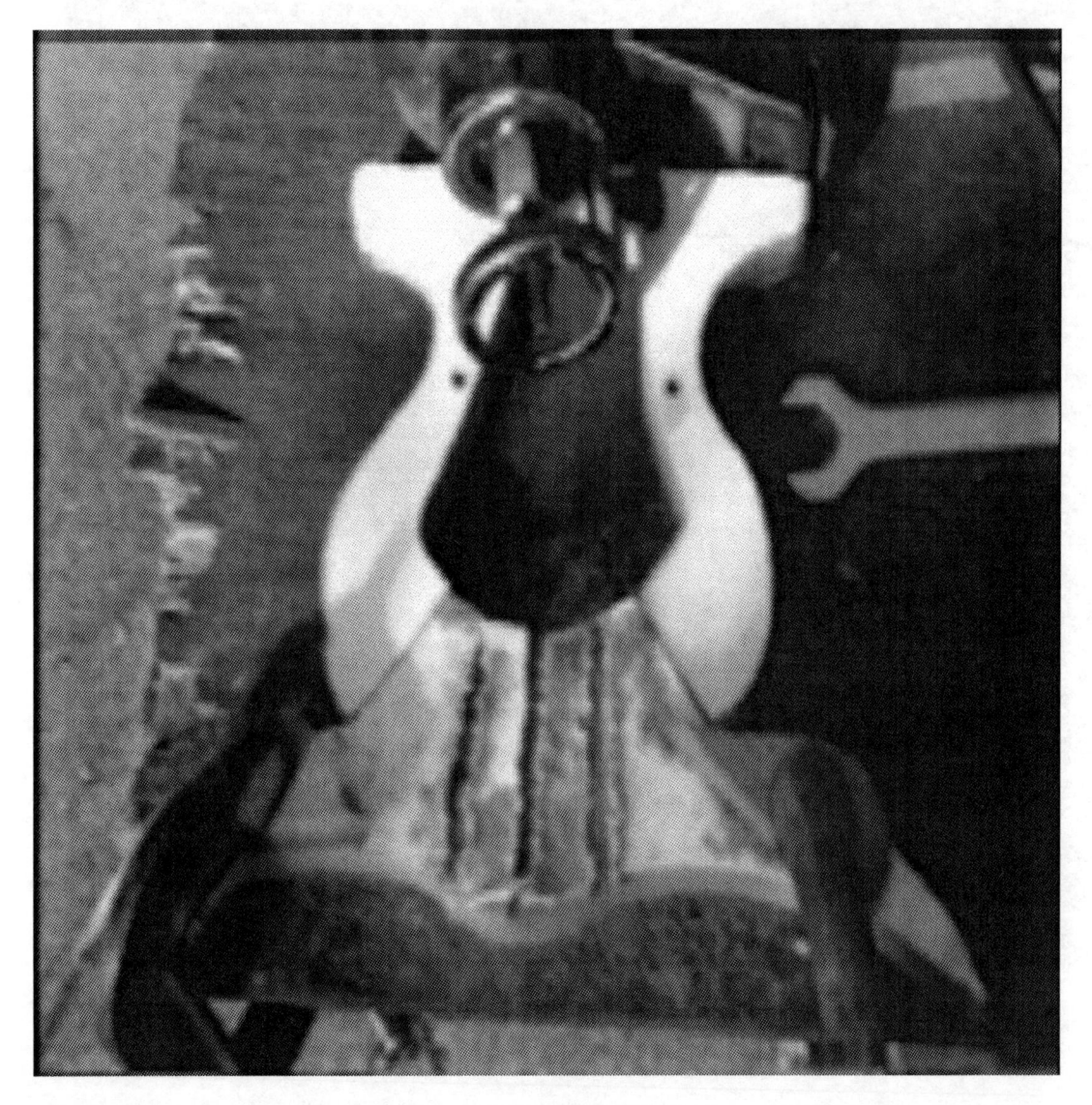

Fig. 1-12: Routing coin slot , dadoes routed. ROTOZIP® Wrench thickness used to set depth of coin slot, 1/8 " . (Fitting of Horns to Horn Section shown See Step 22.) Two clamps used with scraps under clamp surfaces to protect the part.

21a. Alternative to using a straight cutting bit: Position the Horns at a right angle to a flat surface. Cut the coin slot 1/8 " deep using a Sabrecut bit and a straight edge. Starter cuts can be made from both edges, with the ROTOZIP® and a zipbit, which go a long way in preparing the slot for the completion with hand tools.

22. Lay the completed horns on top of the horn section and evaluate the amount of material to be removed from the horn section. Cut the section out, smooth the surfaces and adjust the fit with the completed Horns.

by Joel N. Gessele

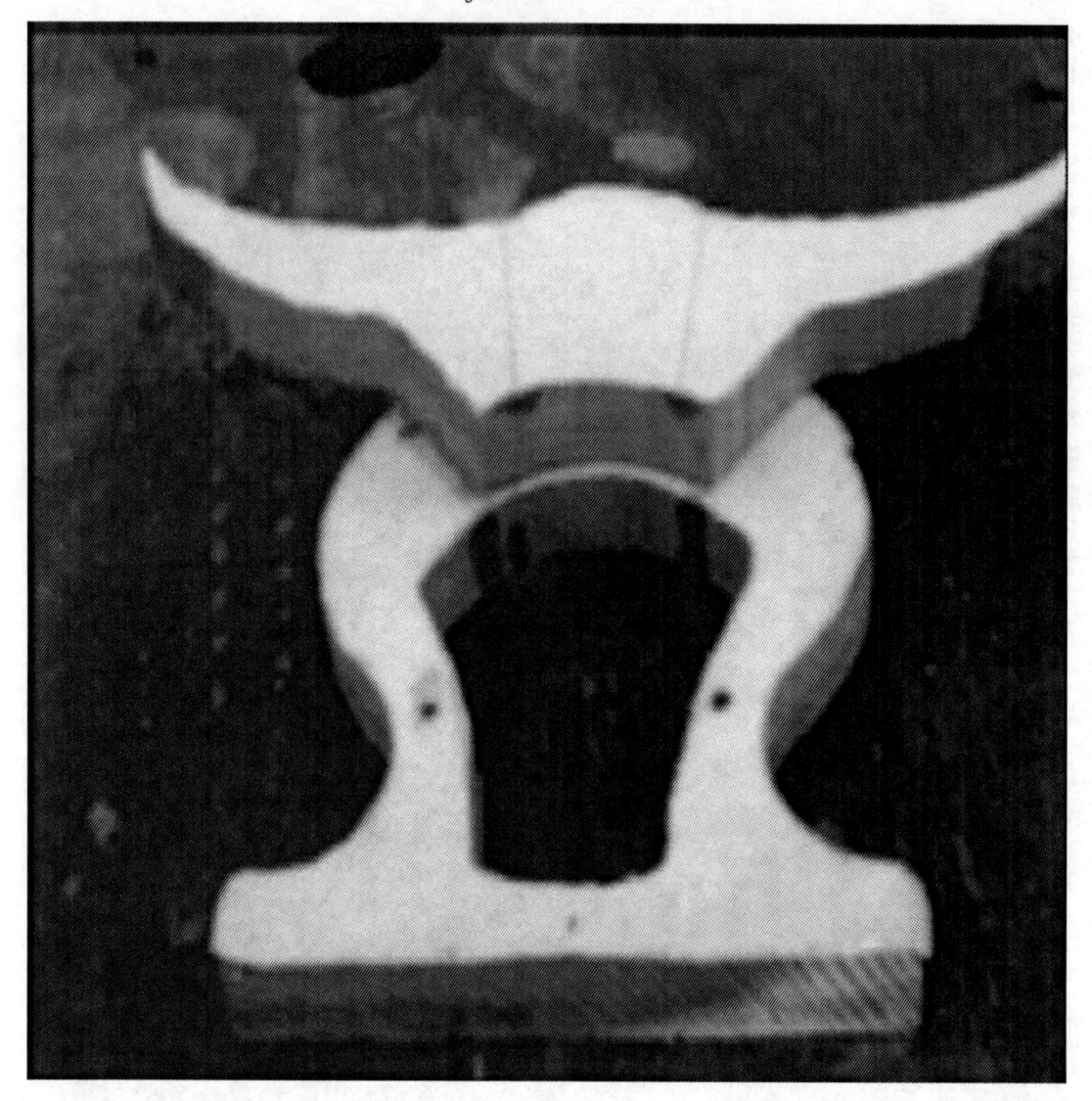

Fig. 1-13: Fitting of Horns in Horn Section. Mark outline of prepared Horns on Horn Section then cut and smooth the surfaces for an outline matching fit.

23. Round over the horn edges with a round over bit.

Fig 1-14: Round over proceeding using part of the residual Horns stock to provide additional support for the ROTOZIP® depth gauge. Residual stock has the right shape to parallel the horn's curve. Residual stock allows the depth gauge to bridge surfaces and horn doesn't drop past the depth gauge ring and get gobbled by the router bit. Parts are clamped to WorkBench with spacers underneath to give clearance for the bearing, washer, and nut on the round over bit. Alternative is to round edges with the rasp.

Bull Wood Bank : Preparation for Assembly

Few experiences are more frustrating than assembling layers of glue covered pieces. The dowel holes are an integral part of the design and cutting process. The holes for the dowels will be the screw holes used to hold the stock to the previous part in the cutting process. Drill out the screw holes and insert dowels to align the parts and hold the part's position during assembly. If contact cement is used rather than wood glue, the dowels can aid in aligning the parts before final contact.

24. Test fit the Face/Head/Horn section/Back

by Joel N. Gessele

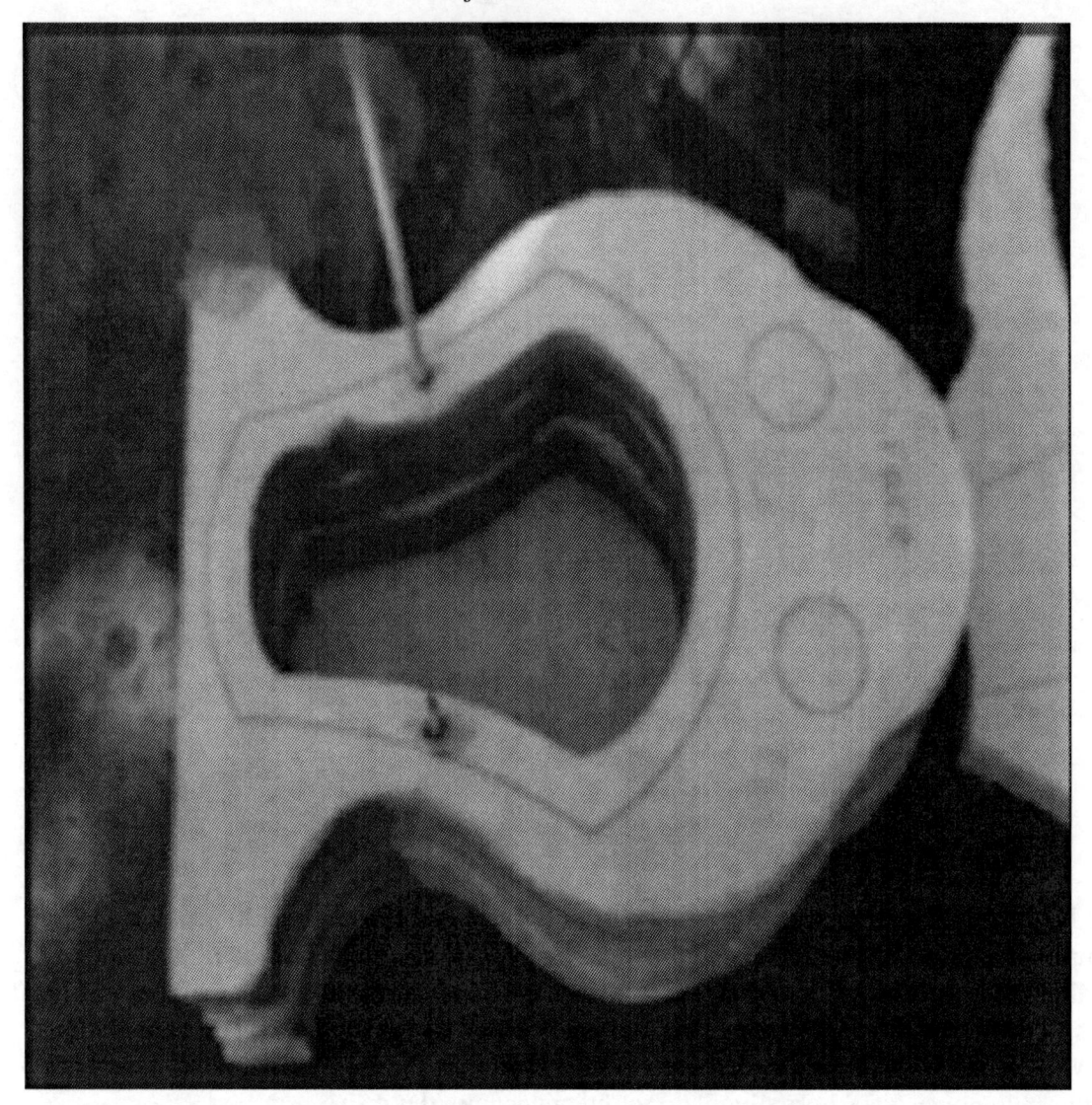

Figure 1-15: First test fit of Head parts, dowels are inserted and will be cut off ¼ " above the surface. Ends of the dowels fit into dowel holes in Bridge (nose) aligning the assemblies preparatory to gluing. Measure the dowels to get a length ¼ " greater than the dowel run in the combined layers. Test fit the Nose sections and make two dowels ¼ " less than the dowel run in the combined layers.

Bull Wood Bank : Assembly

24. Drill the holes for the eyes and nostrils. A forstner bit or spade bit provides a detailed hole .The spade bit at very light pressure is preferred. A twist drill is acceptable, but is not as decorative.

25. Glue the layers and weight or clamp the assemblies. Make two assemblies, the head section and the nose section.

Figure 1-16: Glue up of Head Assembly started. Back and Horn section assembled. Completed Nose Assembly, upper Right.

26. When the glue has set, form the outer surfaces with a belt sander or the 6" rasp. Prepare a smooth stable base. Sand surfaces with sand paper.

27. If the Horns slide into the Horn Section too easily and are easily removed, place a bead of glue along the edge of the coin slot and allow it to dry. If the Horns are still too loose, reapply and/or apply bead on back of horns. The carpenters glue that I used was diluted and resulted in a thin bead, that fortified the edges of the coin slot and several rays in the back. Let the bead dry completely before testing the fit.

28. Round over the back, face, and nose with a round over bit.

29. Test fit the Head and nose assemblies to assure that there is sufficient depth for the dowel stubs. Glue and clamp.

by Joel N. Gessele

Bull Wood Bank : Finish
30 Sign and date the item.

31. Apply a finish, appropriate for the wood and use of the bank. Shellac was used because it can be applied quickly and shellac is nontoxic. It must be allowed to dry completely after the last coat is applied to prevent the horns from sticking in the slot of the head. A coating of Howard's Feed N Wax was used to prevent the shellacked surfaces from bonding.

Bull Wood Bank : Results

The use of the previous part to guide the cut is an attempt to reduce the sanding effort and match the edge of the adjoining section. Using the just completed part as the pattern for the next piece makes a smooth transition between the parts.

The cedar used for this project presents several challenges, it is softer than pine and will chip to break easily. It was used in spite of these known problems to test the ROTOZIP© cutting capabilities. Cedar's lone advantage for this project is that the completed project weighs only one pound -empty-!

A belt sander was used to smooth the edges and base. It is optional, but speeds the work. The lead roller was ideal for the concave curve above the base. It was helpful to sand the subassemblies with a visible corner across the parts. The corner line was sanded to form a right angle with the end surfaces, giving a visual indication that the shaping of the sections is still square with the ends. When the sanding was nearly complete, the corner lines were rounded.

Amber shellac darkened the cedar used for this project. The non-toxic qualities and the ease with which the coats of shellac can be applied are benefits of shellac. Shellac imparts an antique appearance and it can be renovated with sanding and re-application. Shellac can be scratched, clouded when contacted with water, or dissolved when exposed to alcohol. It is easy to rejuvenate.

Taming the ROTOZIP® Spiral Saw

Magazine Box or Scrap Book Holder:

Fig. 2-01: Magazine box: Amber Shellac finish, Unfinished hardwood accent used as part of latching mechanism.

Magazine Box or Scrap Book Holder: Description

The Magazine Box or Scrap Book Holder is a simple cedar / plywood box to organize and protect valued magazines or Scrap Books. The construction materials were chosen from inexpensive materials used with a minimum of processing. The size should be customized to your application. When paired with the same sized boxes, the units interlock and present a flush face.

This project is less complicated than the other box projects and the leftovers from this project are excellent sources of materials for building trays. The Bureau Box Tray and the Bureau Box with six pieces and case splitting are more challenging. The experience gained on this project translates into better results on subsequent projects. The judicious use of materials for this and the next two projects may require setting aside materials for subsequent projects. Review the next two projects for material use suggestions.

Taming the ROTOZIP® Spiral Saw

The maximum internal width of the box is 3" when Super Cedar Closet Lining boards are used. The dimensions used in this plan will hold a 3" three ring binder. Other sizes are easy to plan and the boxes should be sized for their intended contents.

Fig. 2-02: Side and front view of Magazine box.

Magazine box: Materials

Super Cedar Closet Lining.
¼ " Birch Plywood for top and bottom panels.
Glue for joints and fortifying edges
Pressed Wood Medallions for decoration

Magazine box: Tools

1/8" straight cut router bit
Guide point bit for cross cutting and trimming
Framing square or WorkBench (see Appendix)
Circle cutter attachment and Expanded Base (See Appendix)

Magazine box: Plan

The dimensions for this project, enclose a 3" ring binder. The boxes can be set vertically or stacked horizontally. In both situations the cases can be interlocked by fitting the lining's tongue and groove. The 3" ring binder used for this project has external dimensions of 3 "w x 12 " h x 11 ½ " L. Stopped grooves are required on the ends. The stopped grooves are easy to cut on the WorkBench, but they could be cut with the Expanded base and a portable fence or with a straight edge.

Magazine box: Blueprint

Figure 2-03: Blueprint for Magazine Box, Material used is Super Cedar Closet Lining for the case.

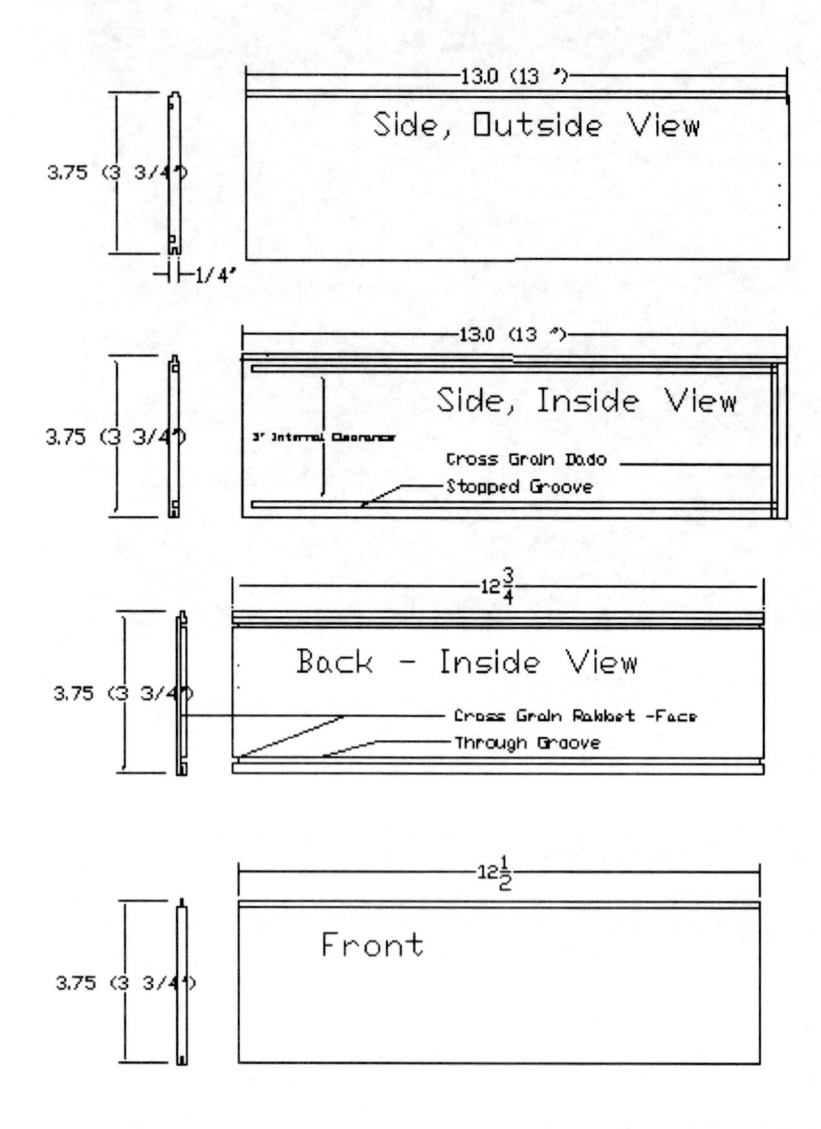

Magazine Box: Cutting

1. Cut Cedar boards to length and plywood panels to length and width. The picture that follows is the beginning squaring cut that uses the clamping bar to guide the ROTOZIP®. The reference lines are used to align the edge. The primary edge of the clamping bar is a right angle to the reference lines.

Fig. 2-04: Cross cutting using the WorkBench, alternative is to use the framing square as a guide to aid in cutting square, straight parts. This project uses the tongue and groove on the Super Cedar Closet lining. It may be desirable to fortify the groove and the inner edge of the tongue with glue. This can be done on the raw stock before the parts are cut to length preserving the tongue and groove during the cutting operations. Cut top and bottom panels.

2. Setup a fence and a 1/8 " straight cut router bit in the Expanded Base. The first cut to be made will be the six grooves to hold the top and bottom panels in the sides and back. Four of the six grooves are stopped grooves so that the unfilled groove does not show on the edge. The 1/8" groove's inner edge is approximately 3/8 " in from the edge on both tongue and groove edges (see Guidepoint edge trimming in the Appendix).

3. Cut the cross grain dadoes on the sides to hold the back. One dado is needed on each side. If desired, you can plan on trimming the ends with the guidepoint bit (see Guidepoint edge trimming in the Appendix) .

4. Adjust the fence to cut the rabbets on the End. Test fit the joint. Check to make sure that the rabbet doesn't bottom out in the dado and that the shoulder fits tightly against the

shoulder of the dado. Transfer the finished width to the top and bottom panels. Two measurements should be checked and transferred, the width and the position of the shoulder. Complete the top and bottom panel rabbets based on the end panel dimension. Remember, the rabbets remove material from the "A" surface (face) of the panel.

5. Cut the front cover panel to length. The front panel is held in place by friction and it can only be adjusted by sanding only if it is long enough.

Magazine box: Preparation for Assembly

6. Dry assemble the 3 sided frame, checking for alignment of the dadoes at the corners, and the orientation of the cross grain dado to the back.

Fig. 2-05: Part layout in preparation for assembly.

6. Slide in the top and bottom panels. Check the overall fit, squareness by measuring the diagonals, and fit along the frame. Adjust if necessary by sanding.

Magazine box: Assembly

7. Disassemble the test assembly, laying the parts in order for re-assembly.

8. Glue cross grain dadoes and back. Add rubber bands to hold and compress the joints. Check to make sure that the grooves for the top and bottom are lined up in the corners.

9. Glue dadoes for top and bottom, slide into place, add rubber bands as clamping. Recheck end fit of frame, check the fit of top and bottom along end and sides.

Magazine box: Finish

10. Trim end joints with guidepoint bit if desired. This step determines the final length.

11. Scrape glue and sand exterior surfaces.

12. Fortify exposed edges of top and bottom panels.

13. Adjust the fit of the front panel, and add a latching mechanism if desired.

14. Remove sanding dust.

15. Sign and date the box.

16. Finish, Shellac according to manufacturer's directions is preferred.

Magazine box: Results

Check the assembly to insure that the box is square. The box made had a twist in it. This was not noticed for several months until the box was set horizontally on a hard flat surface.

The friction fit lid should have a latch. A set of cams to the end panels appear to be the best solution.

by Joel N. Gessele

Bureau Box Tray :

Fig. 3-01: Modern and traditional sized trays. Only four end grain edges per tray.

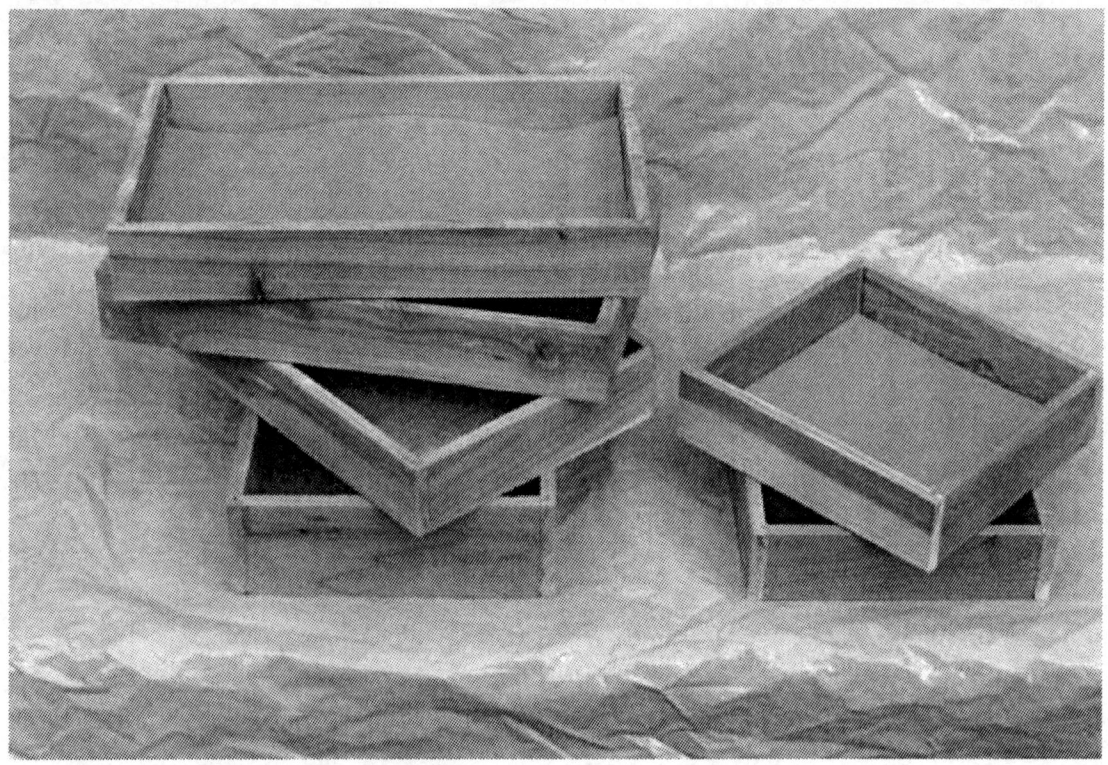

Bureau Box Tray: Description

The Bureau Box Tray is based on small trays that were used in cedar bureau boxes. Most of these trays have become separated from their original boxes. These trays are useful in organizing the contents of Bureau Boxes because they can be placed above the bottom on rails attached to the sides of the boxes or stacked inside the box. Two sizes are listed, one that fits the traditional 5 x 10 Cedar Box and another for the Bureau Box constructed in Project 4.

Four variations of the tray were attempted. First attempt was a stacking design, second used plywood, third variation used solid wood to avoid finger joint problems, and this version avoids the cutting of finger joints, permitting use of either solid wood or plywood. This version exposes only four end grain edges and uses joints that are easy to make. The dimensions allow a lid on the tray or mirror in the lid of the box. The reason for including such a simple project is to present a process and materials that will work when a simple tray is needed. This project is more difficult than the Magazine Box, but not as difficult as the Bureau Box. It uses only a small amount of materials, making it an ideal initiation project.

by Joel N. Gessele

Error 124: Field does not end properly.Bureau Box Tray: Materials

Traditional: for existing 10 x 5 ½ inside dimension Bureau Boxes
    2   3 ¾ x 5 3/8 x ¼ Sides
    2   3 ¾ x 4 ¾   x ¼ Ends
    2   5 1/8 x 4 ¾   x ¼ for Bottoms
Modern: See Project 4.
    2   3 ¾ x 8 5/8 x ¼ Sides
    2   3 ¾ x 5   x ¼ Ends
    2   5   x 8 3/8 x ¼ Bottoms

Bureau Box Tray: Tools
    Circle cutter attachment
    Framing square + C-Clamps, Speed Square + C-Clamps, or Work Bench (see Appendix)
    Work Bench and Expanded Base
    Urethane glue
    6" Rasp
    1/8" Straight cut router bit

Taming the ROTOZIP® Spiral Saw

ROTOZIP® Guidepoint and Sabrecut bits
C-Clamps or rubber bands
Medium and fine grades of sand paper
Pad Sander

Bureau Box Tray: Blueprint
Fig. 3-03:

Bureau Box Tray Side (Inside View)

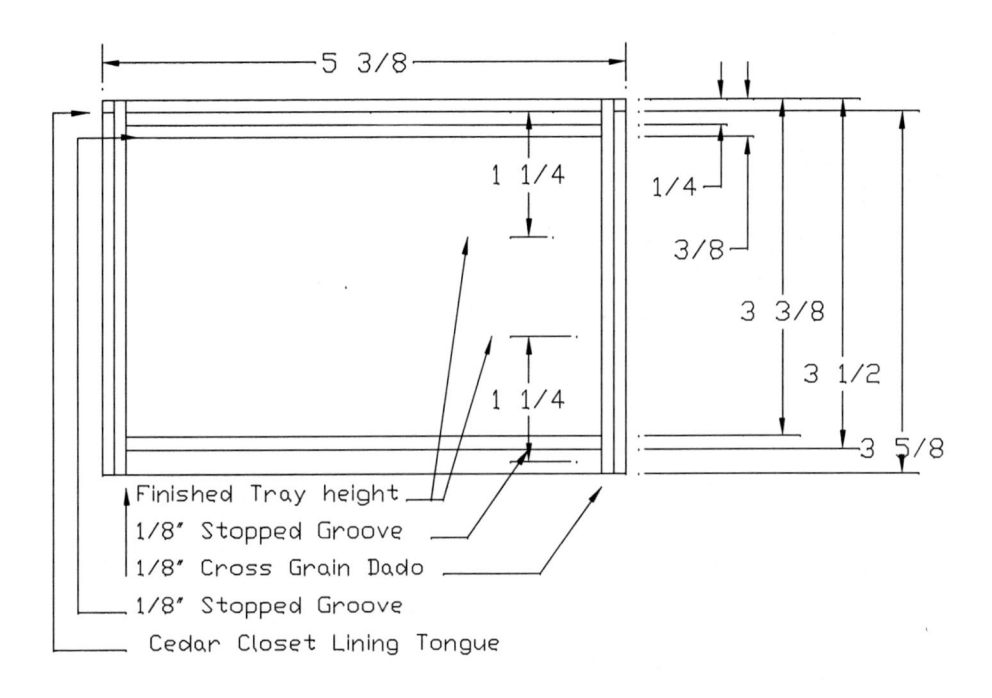

- 5 3/8
- 1 1/4
- 1/4
- 3/8
- 3 3/8
- 1 1/4
- 3 1/2
- 3 5/8
- Finished Tray height
- 1/8" Stopped Groove
- 1/8" Cross Grain Dado
- 1/8" Stopped Groove
- Cedar Closet Lining Tongue

33

by Joel N. Gessele

Bureau Box Tray End (Inside View)

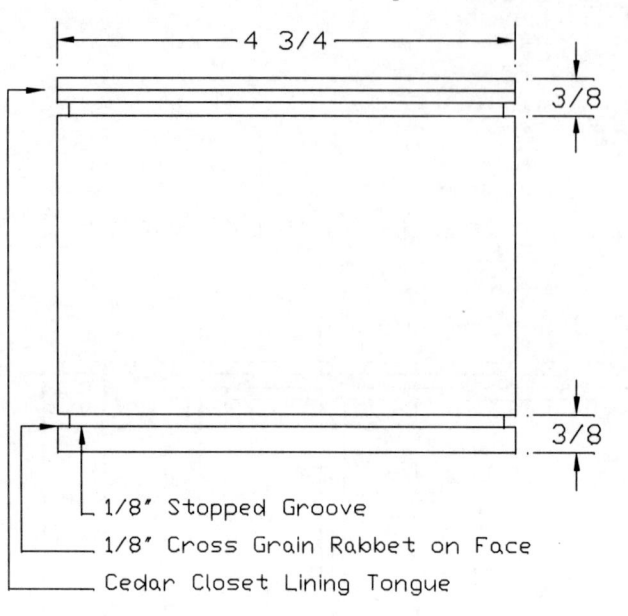

- 4 3/4
- 3/8
- 3/8
- 1/8" Stopped Groove
- 1/8" Cross Grain Rabbet on Face
- Cedar Closet Lining Tongue

Bureau Box Tray Bottom (s) (Face View)

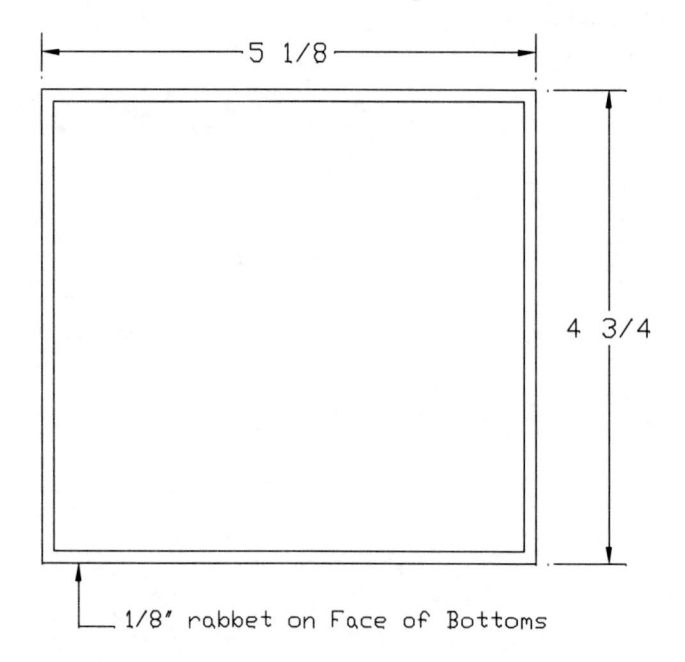

- 5 1/8
- 4 3/4
- 1/8" rabbet on Face of Bottoms

Bureau Box Tray: Cutting

1. Cut stock to length, if the ROTOZIP® is the tool of choice, use a speed square, framing square, or the WorkBench Material Clamp to make right angle cuts. Cut bottoms using a straight edge to guide the ROTOZIP®.

2. Setup a fence and a 1/8 " straight cut router bit in the Expanded Base. The first cuts to be made will be the Eight groove joints on the inside edges of the case parts. The finished joint will be flush trimmed. In an ideal construction, the groove should run at least 1/8" in from the shoulder of the tongue or the end top of the groove. Sufficient material is available for the tray sides to place the dado with some material to trim. Four of the grooves are stopped grooves. Stopped grooves can be made by lowering the stock onto the straight cut bit. Marks on the fence are helpful for guiding the start and stop points of stopped grooves. The cutter depth must be set to remove sufficient material to hold the top and bottom rabbets and only marginally compromise the strength of the part until it is assembled and glued. See Flush Trim Adjustment in the Appendix.

3. Cut the cross grain dadoes in the side parts. These joints will eventually be trimmed using the end as the guide. Sufficient material is needed for a strong shoulder, however specifications must be met or the tray may not fit. To avoid splitting out on the trailing end, back in a notch before starting the major cut. The cross grain dadoes will be trimmed after the assembly's glue has dried. Be sure that the exterior faces of the end panels yields a tray of proper length after the planned trimming.

4. Cut the rabbets on the end part. Although the measurements indicate that half of the thickness is to be removed, it actually looks like a third of it is removed to fit in the cross grain dado in the sides. Remember that the material is removed from the outside surface (face). The blueprints indicate this by showing a notch where the dado and rabbet operations have removed all of the material, a rabbet from one side intersecting a groove on the other.

5. Transfer the dimensions from the case pieces to the bottom panels. Although the bottom parts were cut to length and width, transferring dimensions from the just completed joints precisely define where the shoulder of the rabbet must be cut. The transfer of the actual dimensions is the last chance to adjust the joints to the actual conditions yielding tight joints and minuscule seams.

6. Cut the rabbets on the bottom panels starting with the cross grain cuts. Remember that the material is removed from the outside surface (face).

Bureau Box Tray: Preparation for Assembly

7. Sand all End, Side, and Bottom piece edges. Remove the broken fibers from the routed edges with a wood chisel, razor blade, or rasp.

by Joel N. Gessele

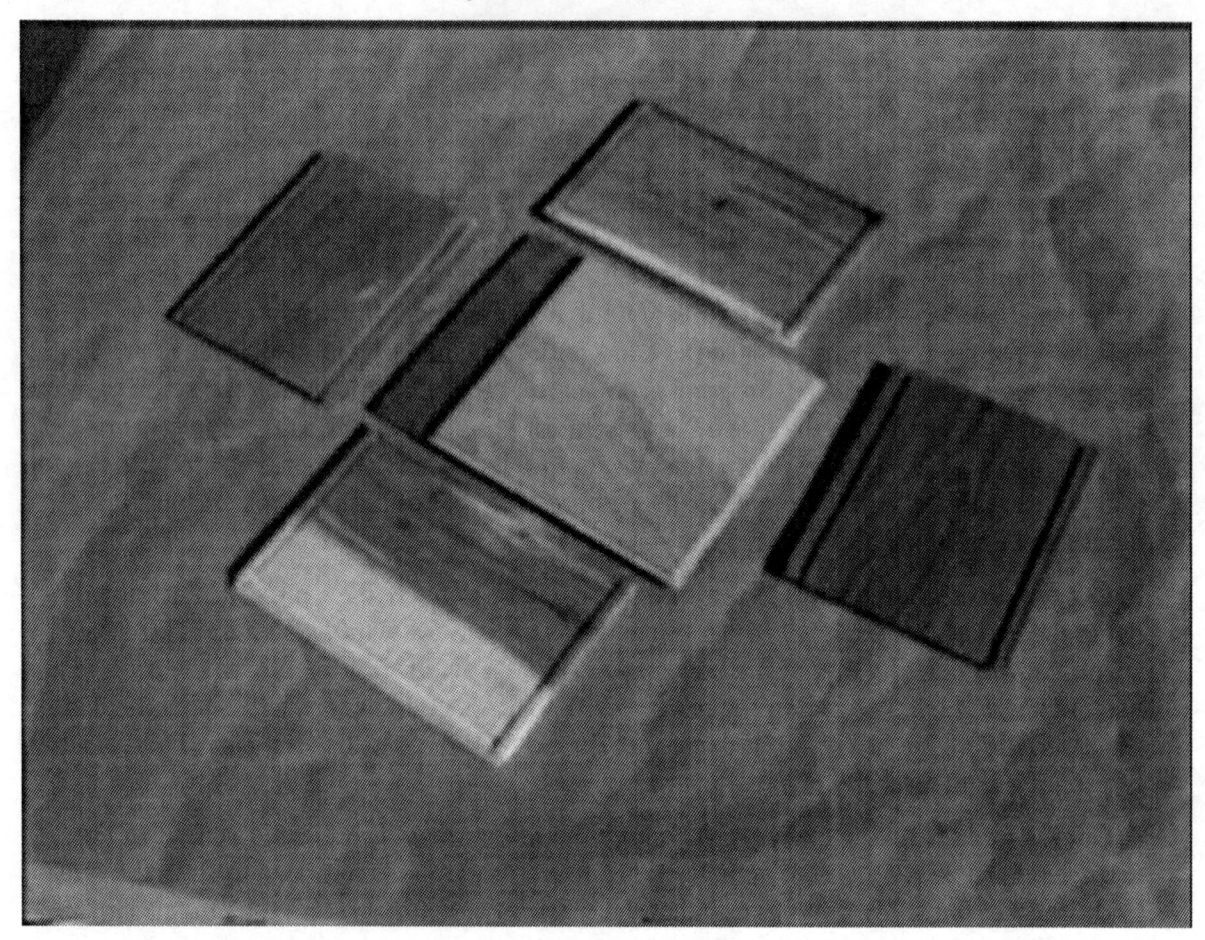

Fig. 3-04: Parts, Top: Side with dadoes, and stopped grooves, 3 O'clock: Ends with grooves but rabbet is face down, Bottom: Side, with dadoes, and stopped grooves, 11 O'clock: End, Middle: two bottoms with rabbets around face edges.

8. Test fit the pieces. Trim by sanding if necessary. Check that the assembly is square when dry assembled. Check all joints.

Fig 3-05: Dry assembly of Traditional sized box to check fit. The Dry Assembly is very important step in the process. It gets really busy when you cover joints with glue and try to get six pieces coordinated.

Bureau Box Tray: Assembly

9. Begin assembly by joining an End to the Sides following the recommendations for use of the glue manufacturer. An expanding urethane glue was used to fill joint voids and adhere to the cedar.

10. Slide in the bottoms, if plywood is used, glue all three edges, (the rabbet and dado touching the two sides and the end).

11. Close off the assembly by putting the other end in place with glue on the joints.

12. Clamp if you have the clamps, otherwise use rubber bands to hold the assembly in place expecting that some places the rubber bands will be glued to the tray and that the panels will hold the frame square.

by Joel N. Gessele

13. When the glue has dried, remove clamps and rubber bands.

14. Place a guide point bit in the ROTOZIP®, and trim the tongue and groove from the bottoms and ends.

Fig. 3-06: Edge trimming of tray ends. Excess side panel and glue are removed without undue compression of end panel by the guidepoint bit. Glue and excess material is being removed, try to use the minimum amount of pressure to avoid marking the panel where the guidepoint surface touches the panel, and avoid pressure that would round the corner.

Fig. 3-07: Edge trimming of groove from case bottom. Start the cut along the bottom of a side. The end -- bottom has been trimmed, the small tab will be removed as well as the Super Cedar groove and the excess glue. Neat!

by Joel N. Gessele

Fig. 3-08: Tab trimmed and flush trimming of the bottom is proceeding. Note the tendency of the cedar to split along the grain line.

15. Using the Sabrecut bit, cut the tray to 1 ¼ " height using a fence or a straight edge.

Taming the ROTOZIP® Spiral Saw

Fig. 3-09: Case splitting with left to right cut and portable fence installed on the Expanded base in the WorkBench.

Fig. 3-10: Cutting second tray to 1 ½ " height. Also visible is the excess urethane glue.

Fig. 3-11: Results of Case splitting, second case cut to size, and initial preparation of one tray with chisel and rasp. Tray on left is trimmed. Diamond in the middle is the excess from two trimming operations.

16. Cut the other tray to the 1 ¼ " height.

17. Rasp the tray edges, scrape glue excess, and sand to ease edges and remove glue.

Bureau Box Tray: Finish
18. Sign and date the trays.

19. Most trays are unfinished, a felt pad in the bottom is a nice accessory.

Bureau Box Tray: Results
The Bureau Box Trays use a small amount of material and have immediate application in existing Bureau Boxes with tray rails or when set in the bottom. Bureau Box trays are unfinished, a felt pad in the bottom is a nice accessory.

by Joel N. Gessele

Trays for second series of 8 trays needed to be ½ " longer than the set made for the original box. Although the trays are meant to be made before the Bureau Box, their size must fit the finished Bureau box. Consider making the traditionally sized tray before making trays for an unmade Bureau box. Length for this series of trays was 9". The time to prepare the case parts was 3.5 hours. The time to cut, rabbet top/bottom panels, and dry assemble 1.5 hours. Gluing took 2 hours. Edge trimming, sanding of the resulting cubes, and case splitting took 2 hours. About two hours was spent removing the excess glue from the inside edges and corners (all exterior glue is removed by edge trimming or sanding).

It may seem extremely retentive to give detailed directions on case splitting, but you might as well get the benefit of previous experience. Previously, the sabrecut bit would leave gouges in the edge when control of the case splitting process lapsed. One method to remove the gouges would be to fine tune the edge trim with a second cut that trims a 1/16" from the edge. This may encourage splitting along grain lines, making the results worse. I tried to control the case splitting operation holding only the 1 ¼ " wide section of the cube. WRONG. Use the whole cube, only the last cut, opening the cube, needs extra caution to avoid compressing the case. The case splitting technique was improved by allowing 5/16" of the sabrecut bit above the expanded base. Three advantages resulted when a minimum bit exposure was used, the decreased the length of exposed bit is safer, the shoulder that results when a cut is started on an edge is smaller, and more of the glue(urethane) overflow is still in place stabilizing the case as it is split. Usually a Rosendahl case splitting operation fills the kerf with an 1/8" shim on completed edges for the final edge cut.

The case splitting seemed to be most controllable when the cut is made **right to left**. The resulting case will have a rough edge that can be removed by running the edges past the bit from **left to right** stabilizing the tray using the edge on the expanded base and bottom of the tray as an additional surface to stabilize the trim cut. The second tray from the cube can be cut using the bottom and the edges to guide the cutting. Concerned about the final appearance of the tray, I became too focused on the tray and didn't use the whole cube to control the cut or the bottom of the tray as another surface to control the trim to size operation. The very simple acts of using the entire case to guide the case splitting operation, using the bottom and edges as the surfaces to hold onto the tray, and a reverse pass to tune up the edge resulted in perfect trays with smooth even edges.

The diagonals of A L L of the resulting trays were between 10 3/8" and 10 7/16". The diagonals were not checked during glueing/clamping. I am elated that the procedures produce consistent, precise results without extreme attention to individual measurements.

by Joel N. Gessele

Bureau Box:

Fig. 4-01: Bureau Box , Hasp attached temporarily, surface reflections from background

Bureau Box: Description

The Bureau Box is a cedar box reminiscent of the 1930's gift boxes used for gifts of candy and nuts. The subsequent use of the box was to store and protect scarves, handkerchiefs, gloves, stationary, or as a jewelry box. This version utilizes aromatic cedar to continue the traditional uses for these boxes. Brass hardware was added to embellish the box and allow securing the contents with a padlock. The rich colors, knots, and grain of the cedar plus the brightness of the brass creates a functional and decorative jewel.

A traditional Bureau Box has the internal dimensions of 10 " by 5 ½ " and various depths. The dimensions for this version have been modernized (made larger) and adjusted to make use of the cedar materials. The interior dimensions have been increased to accommodate 8.5 x 11 sheets of paper, permitting use as a document box, a linen storage box, a jewelry box of moderate capacity, or a keepsake organizer. A tray rail has been included in the plan to accommodate Bureau Box Trays on the tray rail at the upper level and stack trays in the bottom. Two trays can be placed at the upper level on the tray rail. Plans for this size tray are included in the Bureau Box Tray Project directions as the modern version. The tray

Taming the ROTOZIP® Spiral Saw

project was placed before the Box project because the trays are simpler, used less material, and the traditional sized trays can be used in existing cedar boxes.

Fig. 4-02: Bureau Box -inside view no trays, 8 ½ x 11 paper in bottom.

The wood for this project is the George C. Brown Super Cedar Closet lining. Larger panels are used requiring that the panels be glued prior to cutting. Two boards are glued together for the case, three boards for the top and bottom. Occasionally a box of the Closet lining will have boards cut from the same raw stock. When these consecutive boards are used for the case, the upper band and the lower band have similar grain patterns. If the sequential boards are four feet long there is enough material to make all the vertical sections of the case from the same panel. Dry assemble the panels to make sure that all of the "A" sides are used. "B" sides may look fine, but they are likely to have planer marks that will show up when the surface is sanded or finished.

by Joel N. Gessele

A two board panel was used because a single board box seemed to be too small. Two of the pictures seem to distort the actual height of the completed box. The actual height is 7 1/8 " and the inside depth is 4 ¾ inches. Adjust the height of the upper case by re-cutting the case. The lid, at 1", is lightweight and head space is partially filled with tray when closed. These dimensions still allow for a mirror in the lid or a cover on the tray. A 3 ¾ " high item can be placed inside below the tray(s). If you want the trays to be level with the edge, lower the tray rail.

A case made from the ¼ " closet lining material appears to be strong enough for this application, in spite of the tongue and groove joint being at the same height all around the case. The completed case is solid and does not deflect with moderate hand pressure. The resulting case weighs 2 ¾ pounds without hardware. A case and four trays weigh 4 pounds. The case, being made from ¼ " material limits the selection of hardware. The screws that come with the hardware may need to be substituted with ¼ " long screws.

The top and bottom panels were glued from three boards. This was done to reduce the number of pieces to handle during the wet assembly. The critical cutting operation is on the rabbet that goes around the top and bottom panels. The rabbet must match the case dimensions and the shoulder must be square. Attention to this part and meticulous adjustment of it determines quality of the Bureau Box's final appearance. The steps for cutting grooves and dadoes progresses from those that are the longest distance from an edge to the rabbets on the edges. The steps complete the critical joints and uses them to make sure that the panels are crafted to the correct dimensions. The materials list does not contain the panel widths because it is expected that the closet lining is the expected choice of materials.

A problem occurred on one of the eight instances where the edge trimming process followed the intersecting panel groove. It was only noticeable on one of the eight instances, so be aware that it could happen when edge trimming. The indentation was small enough to be removed during sanding and the seam adds an interesting detail to the case and cover.

The end grain of the top and bottom (rabbet) is glued to a side panel (groove - along the grain), causing concern that the corners will be pushed out when the panel expands. I checked twenty antique cedar boxes and found that there were examples of split corners. The splitting was not close to the top and bottom panels. Cracks were found at the case corners where the shoulder of the dado cracked.

The materials and construction techniques offer opportunities to improve the appearance as construction proceeds. Trimming the tongue from the cedar yields a precise corner on the very visible lid. Edge trimming the case ends cleans up imperfections on the case corners. The option to scroll the bottom of the case, green line on drawing, could be used to enhance the appearance. The philosophy for building a case this way permits errors to be corrected as construction proceeds. It also may allow a defect to be introduced as the case is made. An example of a construction introduced defect, is the splitting of a corner when trimming the tongue off the top of the case. The glued joint and fortified edges were used to reduce the introduction of construction defects. Finally, the new construction permits the finishing process to lavish attention on the project without hardware to obstruct the application of finish.

A lid retention bracket was not readily available. The wood one included in the plan was used to avoid putting screws in the case and lid. This design gets its strength from its attachment to the case. When the bracket is glued to the case, make sure that the side where the sash chain is inserted into the bracket is covered with glue. The lower bracket may break when test fitting the sash chain. If it breaks, glue the break and attach it to the case. The loop on the sash chain may need to be compressed to fit in the bracket, a diagonal cutter was used as a pliers to place the chain in the bracket.

The blueprint has a green line for a cutout at the base. This cutout was not made on the first Bureau Box. The cutout was not done because the trimming of the tongue and groove occasionally split pieces out. The cutout can be added later, after some experiments are done for making a cutout under comparable conditions. Without the cutout and with another panel, the space underneath could become a concealed compartment.

Fig. 4-03: Bureau box back and side view. Background reflections on part of top and back.

Bureau Box: Materials
Super Cedar Closet Lining   4 feet of 2 boards glued together (case), 2 feet of 3 boards (top and bottom) glued together.
    Qty. Length   Description
      2 -11 ¾ "   Front/Back; (2 Board Panel)

by Joel N. Gessele

```
2 -  9 ¼ "    End; (2 Board Panel)
2- 11 ½ "    Top and bottom (3 Board Panel, trimmed to 9 ¼ " width)
2- 11 ¼ x ¼ x ¼ Tray rails.
4            hinges,
4            corners , if desired,
2            handles,
1            clasp,  optional see instructions for alternative
```
Length of brass sash chain
6 - #18 x ½ Escutcheon Pins (to hold tray rail)
Urethane Glue

Bureau Box: Tools

Gallon jugs and rubber bands(3.5" x 1/4)
Expanded base for ROTOZIP® and WorkBench
Framing square or WorkBench with material clamp.
1/8" straight cut router bit
1/4" straight cut router bit
ROTOZIP® Guidepoint and Zip bits (both are required).
Wood Chisel
6" rasp
Sand paper, sander
Handsaw.
5/16 " drill bit, drill

Bureau Box: Plan

The Bureau Box was made to show that it is possible to make medium sized projects. The dimensions are based on a size that could hold a sheet of paper, envelopes, or moderately sized trays. The first steps are to select the boards to be used for the panels. The cedar closet lining pack should be left intact until you start the project to keep the individual pieces straight. Some boards may have damaged edges or knot holes, however the small diameter logs that are the source for the boards, yield interesting grain patterns not available in wood from other sources.

The panels are glued up first. The two board panel for the case is given priority because the cases final dimensions will be used to fine tune the dimensions of the three board top and bottom panels. Consider cutting the grooves and dadoes as offsets from a pair of primary edges. Cutting the grooves and dadoes as offsets will correct for variations in the width and length of the rough cut panels. Using these procedures, multiple boxes that are the same size, square, and have precise joints can be made easily and consistently.

All the material in the panels is used for case parts, rails, and reinforcement. A small allowance has been allowed for split edges and still complete a case from a 2 board four foot panel and a two foot three board panel.

Bureau Box: Blueprint

Fig. 4-04 Profile and Front/Back Panels

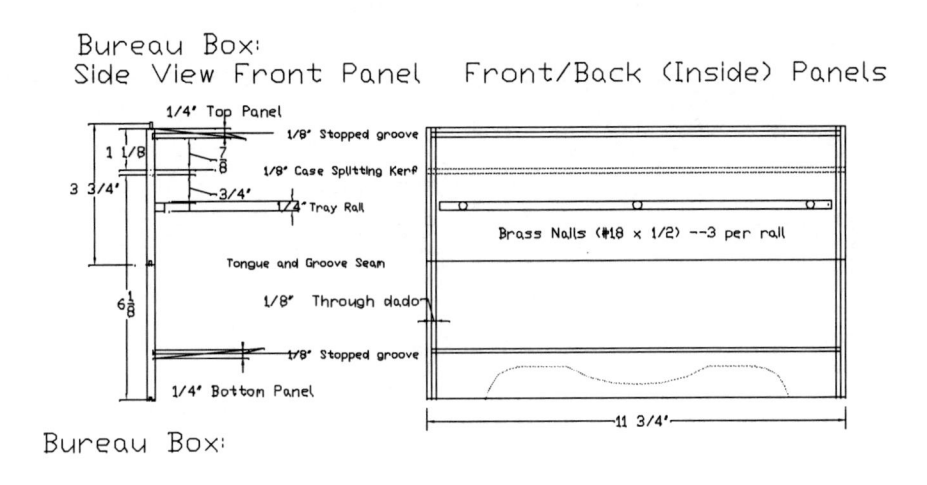

by Joel N. Gessele

Fig. 4-05: Side and Top/Bottom Panels

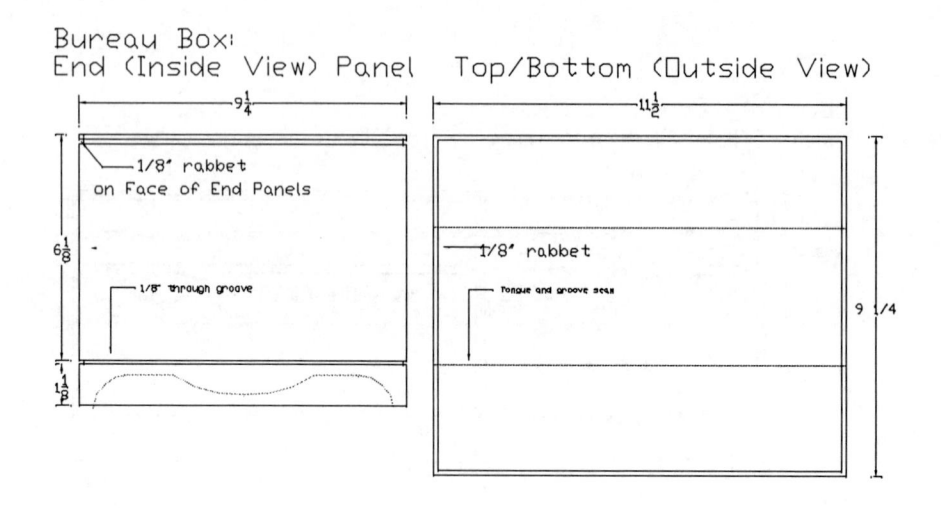

Fig. 4-06: Accessories

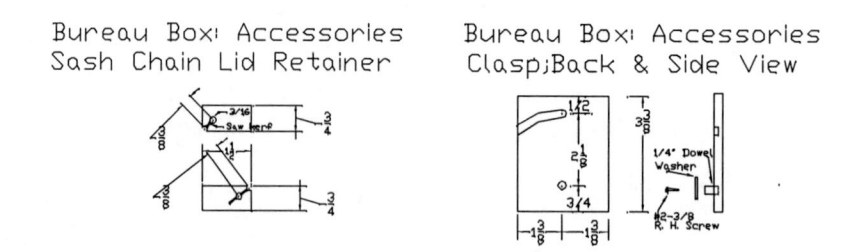

52

Bureau Box: Cutting

1. Select and glue up the 2 board, 4 foot stock for the case and the 3 board 2 foot stock for the top/bottom. Assuming that you don't have a lot clamps, try the following: Dry fit the boards. Lay them out on a flat surface where you can access both ends preferably on a sheet of wax paper (cereal box liners can be used when the roll type is depleted). Apply glue to grooves on the boards and fit together. Weight the boards with two or three filled gallon jugs. Put rubber bands around the boards. Do not allow the weights to release the boards or they may collapse side to side. Add a sufficient number of rubber bands to assure that the tongue and groove joint is tight and glue fills the voids. Avoid glue spills and excessive glue on the "A" sides of the panels. The glue spills may contact the panel and leave a spot on your panel. Although excess glue can be removed by scraping and sanding, it will require additional work to remove from the seam.

2. After the glue has cured, as recommended by the manufacturer, sand the back (interior of the case), and front (exterior), cut the stock for the case to length (two pairs or parts). Check the dimensions of the case pieces and cut the top/bottom parts (one pair of parts). Use the material fence on the WorkBench to guide the ROTOZIP®. Mark the cut with the framing square. Check the fence with the ROTOZIP®, aligning the ROTOZIP® at the ends of the cut. Check the alignment with the spacer bar (see Appendix) and the depth guide notches that mimic the Spiral Saw bit at the edges of the ROTOZIP® depth gauge. Either the Sabrecut bit or the Guidepoint bit can be used. The excess width of the top/bottom is a source of the tray rails   You may prefer to remove material from both sides of the 2 foot panel, making a board centered in the middle of the panel.

by Joel N. Gessele

Fig. 4-07: Trimming Panel for ¼ " tray rails and to center board in rough dimension panel. Cut is right to left and fence (right) clamped to WorkBench is used.

3. Cut the stopped grooves on the fronts and through grooves on the sides. The groove for the bottom has the largest offset and is the best place to start. A straight cut router bit is used for the 1/8" dadoes and rabbets. The direction of the cut is critical to getting a straight dado. The cutting action must pull the ROTOZIP® against the fence.
4. The second cut is the groove for the top in the four case parts. The tongue will be cut off the case parts when the sides and ends are cut flush with the top. If the groove is too close to the edge, a ghost line of the tongue will remain after the edge is trimmed flush with the top.

5. The third cut is the cross grain dado in the front/back. Four are required and instead of multiple minute adjustments, plan on edge trimming the excess with the guidepoint bit along the end.
Caution: Make this cut close to specifications. Although you will trimming the cut to make the outside of the case smooth, the top/bottom dimensions must be adjusted for these dadoes.

6. The fourth series of cuts are the rabbets on the end pieces. The most difficult part of this step is to remember to cut the rabbet on the side opposite to the top/bottom panel grooves.

7. Test fit the case, checking to make sure that the shoulders of the rabbets fit tightly to the shoulders of the dadoes. Adjust the fit before cutting the rabbets around the top/bottom parts.

8. Transfer the actual dimensions from the front and end parts to the top/bottom parts for the rabbet at the edges. Cut the rabbet and check the fit, preparatory to final assembly. The preparation for Assembly rechecks these joints. A check at this time permits immediate correction.

9. Attach the tray rails to the front and back of the case. Three nails are used to hold the rails in place while the glue cures.

10. Cut rectangles for the lid retainer. Drill 5/16 " holes in the rectangles for the sash chain. Cut the kerf for the sash chain in the rectangles using a hand saw. The kerf must be wide enough for the sash chain, a hacksaw kerf is too small.

Bureau Box: Preparation for Assembly

11. Assemble the case and adjust the parts for fit by filing or sanding. Check the joints for fit of the rabbets's shoulder against the side and end. Check this fit on end panels and top/bottom panels. Check the fit in both solitary and when several parts are assembled. Check to make sure that the rabbet doesn't bottom out in the groove or dado and force the shoulder of the rabbet away from side of the panel. Check the corners of front/back panels to side panels to make sure that the grooves align and will allow the top/bottom panel to fit in the corner A loose fit is acceptable, the top/bottom panels and shoulders of the rabbets aid in keeping the case square during and after the glue up step.

A correctable defect would be a groove that is not deep enough because it wasn't held down when cut. Another defect that might be found and corrected is a rabbet where the shoulder drifts out in the center and must be re-cut to make it straight and fit the groove in the panel.

12. Disassemble the case and layout the parts so that they can be assembled with glue in a familiar sequence.

Bureau Box: Assembly

13. The final assembly is best accomplished in steps. This is a larger project and a flawless final appearance is the objective. Assembly of one end helps in making the project flawless by allowing you to concentrate on two joints. Glue up the cross cut dadoes on one end of the case. Put the end pieces on the case, one with glue the other dry. Place rubber bands around the end. This will tax the rubber bands, be careful when putting the bands in place, some may break. Check the end joints for fit on the end, alignment of the dadoes at the inside corners, and square the case with a square.

by Joel N. Gessele

14. After the glue has cured, remove the rubber bands. Remove any excess glue from the grooves. Apply glue to the grooves for the top and bottom panels on the case and assemble the case with the top and bottom. Put glue in the dadoes of the front and back for the end. Put glue in the dadoes of the End for the top and bottom panels and assemble. Check the end joint fit and add rubber bands as needed to eliminate gaps at the end joint and along the body of the case.

15. After the glue has cured, set up the ROTOZIP® with the Guidepoint bit, Expanded Base, and the work bench. Trim the top and ends.

16. Sand the exterior surfaces of the case.

Fig 4-10: Sanding of case, appearance of raw, purple, aromatic cedar before finishing. Color is photoreactive and becomes brown after exposure to sunlight. Photo also shows results of the case splitting. Boards used for this case were sequential cuts and the grain pattern is similar in the upper and lower boards.

17. Change out the Guidepoint bit to a Sabrecut bit. The Sabrecut bit will chatter and create a kerf that is wider than 1/8". Set up a fence 6 1/8" from the sabrecut bit and split the case, cutting the case from left to right.

18. Smooth the edges of the lid and base of the case. Start with a rasp, the Sabrecut bit will leave a shoulder at the entry point and the edge will be rough.

19. Continue with the surface preparation, including the sanding of the interior. Glue the lid retainer brackets in lid and case. As the sanding proceeds, it will be necessary to protect the sanded surfaces by cushioning the surfaces after they have been sanded. Place the completed surfaces only on cloth cushions to prevent the sanding operations from marring an opposite completed surface.

20. Mark and drill holes for the hinges, corners, hasp, and handles. Re-sand the areas where the holes were drilled.

21. If a wooden clasp is desired, layout the clasp on a template. Drill holes through the template and halfway into the back of the clasp. A ¼ " brad point drill bit is preferred for the dowel holes. Glue a dowel into the bottom clasp hole. When the glue is dry, put the dowel through the hole in the template. Trim the dowel flush with the back surface of the template. Drill a hole in the center of the dowel. Fortify the drill hole and top of the dowel with crazy glue. Drill a hole through the case using the template as a guide for the lower clasp dowel. Using the template, drill a hole into the lid for a dowel. Glue a dowel into the hole in the lid. Mark and rout the channel on the back of the clasp material. Shape and decorate the clasp as desired. Pictures of the clasp show dowels through the clasp. Try to stop the drilling process before it goes through the stock.

by Joel N. Gessele

Fig. 4-08: Template made in conjunction with Clasp.

Note: It is assumed that the template thickness is the same as the case. The clasp operation can be tested before the case is molested by mocking up the clasp on the template. Drilling the hole in the lid assumes that the final assembly position can be held. A wood clasp increases customization options.
Note: Cut the dowels with a box knife by rotating the dowel on the edge or rolling the dowel on a hard surface with the knife. The ends of the dowel are smooth, rounded with a majority of the end burnished.

Bureau Box: Finish

22. Sign and date the box.

23 The prototype was finished with shellac. Amber shellac was used to enhance the antique appearance of the box. The resultant coloration is quite pronounced. The inside was not covered, but the case edge, lid edge, and the exterior bottom were covered. The shellac was cut to less than a 1 pound cut. My objective was to get a smooth finish. Cutting the shellac to this degree, can aid in obtaining a smooth finish but a coat of shellac must eventually be applied in single pass. As coats accumulate, a missed area or a run cannot be corrected with another pass and all errors must be sanded off when the coat has dried. However, the result of about 6 coats, is a deep coloration, with a glossy surface, and a tactile reward. Coats of shellac dry quickly and several can be applied in the same afternoon. Starting with a dilute cut will make a base that does not form drips and runs that must be sanded smooth, however a light sanding with fine paper was done between the last coats. The sanding operation was used to examine the projects for dried drips and runs. After sanding, the sanding dust was removed. The sage advice for using shellac as a finish seems to be redundant, thin coats of thin (dilute) shellac.

Bureau Box: Results

When the individual parts were cut, the results were encouraging because the pairs of parts were square and their lengths matched. I had expected that problems would occur because the part pairs were individually cut and that they might not be square. The attention and caution in cutting individual parts included careful marking of the cut line wit the framing square, lightly with a sharp round pencil and checking the cutter position at both sides of the panel before making the cut. The 1/8 " notch inside the depth gauge is an excellent reference. The cut should be completed with the same point on the depth gauge touching the fence and the depth gauge flat on the panel.

The sequence of steps had not been established when this project was done and it lead to some changes that will make the joints fit better and reduce setup time. Even with these problems, the lid of the first case could be rotated 180 degrees and it still matched the case.

If parts are not square, correct the problem as soon as the problem is noticed. Corrective action may take the form of squaring the parts or selecting primary edges and making subsequent cuts as offsets from those edges. Eight of the twelve edges can be trimmed after assembly. This should allow most projects to end with captivating results. Hand trimming of the corner of the panel may be required because the panel is released before the cut is complete and the panel must be caught to prevent it from falling to the ground. Take precautions to protect panels as they are cut, they are cabinet parts, not cordwood. A tab at the end of a panel can be removed by sanding or with the 6 inch rasp.

When you glue the case and top/bottom panels, use enough rubber bands to force the boards together and remove any warpage that may be present in the board. Weight the panels to prevent them from folding up under the pressure of the bands. Wipe off the excess glue, from the A side seams. If there is too much glue, the seam can be redefined with a straight edge, counter sink bit, and ROTOZIP®. Weight the panels to align the panel

by Joel N. Gessele

faces, removing any step between panels caused by looseness in the fit of the tongue and groove joint.

The instructions assume that the parts are square when the grooves, dadoes and rabbets are cut, if they aren't, compensate by assigning primary edges and make the cuts based on that edge. Example: If a side is not square, select the squarest corner and make all of the cuts with these edges against the fence. The excess material, including the out of square material can be removed by flush trimming .

A second series of 4 boxes was made using the instructions. The cases were split using the Rosendahl method for case splitting and grooves were cut as offsets from the bottom edge. The Rosendahl method for case splitting yields a raised edge inside lower case and a wrap around step inside the cover. The variations represented in this set of four boxes, include:
- o   Four variations of handles.
- o   Decorative cut bottom on one box
- o   Locking Latches on two boxes
- o   Tear Drop Hinges on two boxes
- o   Rounded edges versus original square edge on four boxes
- o   Rosendahl case splitting on four boxes

The first steps in preparing the case for Rosendahl case splitting are grooves 1/8 " x 1/8" x 6 1/4" from the bottom. The grooves follow the same plan as the grooves that hold the top/bottom panels. The grooves are stopped grooves on the front/back and through grooves on the end panels ON THE INSIDE. Prepare at least one scrap piece as a story board for the grooves. The grooves will be concealed inside the glued up box and the breaching the case requires that a corner of the router bit .must intercept the inside groove

After the box is assembled, glued, sanded, prepared for splitting, position fences to allow cutting a 1/8 x 1/8 " groove at 6 1/8 " from the bottom edge. Two fences are suggested to prevent the box from wandering during the case splitting operation. If you are extremely careful you can hold the case against the fence and obtain a straight cut. The additional security of two fences is preferred to avoid adding unplanned decorative features. See Fig: 4-09. If the bottom of the case is used as the primary edge, the glue overflow in the inside corners will hold the lid in place until all four sides are cut. My external cut was slightly over 6 1/8 from the bottom and a pencil line width of the intersecting grooves could be seen after each side was cut.

Taming the ROTOZIP® Spiral Saw

Fig: 4.09. Case splitting artifact, internal edge is visible, artifact provides a key for orienting the lid on closure. Fortunately, the case split in the middle and only a little trimming was needed to allow the lid to open and close easily. Also visible is the corner treatment, the corners were rounded by creating a 1/32" facet and sanding it so that no corner line was visible. The original Bureau Box left the corners and edges square, making the brass corners fit nicely on the lid of the original box.

The Rosendahl case splitting method can make a tight fitting lid even with 1/8 " straight cut bits. If the depth is greater than half the depth on either cut a looser fit is obtained. If you want to use hinges the looser fit is desirable. If you make the lids precisely, no hinge or latch is needed to hold the lids in place. The edges of the case and lid were fortified with crazy glue and the edges were covered with shellac. Try to cover only the case edges and not the sides. If a little shellac flows over the edge onto the surface, the additional will appear as additional coats near the case split and may look like a run in the shellac. Amber Shellac was used, ten coats, 4 initial in one afternoon w/o sanding between coats because no runs or drips were created, sanding after drying overnight, two coats, sanding after drying overnight, two coats, sanding, two coats. Shellac was thinned approximately 1 to 3. The shellac was so thin that no runs or drips occurred in the first four coats. The first runs occurred when I tried to leave too much shellac on the top and runs down the edge occurred.

by Joel N. Gessele

The hinges and latches for Rosendahl split cases must move the screws back from the edge. A teardrop hinge was used and a locking latch was found where the attachment holes were back from the edge enough to get the screws back from the case splitting rabbets. The alternative is to make tight fitting lids or straight cut case splits. There are advantages to both methods. Pictures on the variations of the boxes are included to allow you to form a preference.

There were a great variety of grain patterns and colors in this box of Cedar Closet Lining. One case was made with a book matched set of boards, two were from consecutive cuts from the same stock, and all the tops were from an intricately figured three board set. The bottoms were cut from the two foot lengths in the box after they were glued up in three board panels.

Fig. 4-10: Upper right: original with wood latch and metal handles. Lower right: Friction fit lid, carved wood handle. Lower center: Locking latch, Oval handle. Lower Left: Tear Drop Hinge, wood handle Decorative cut bottom. Upper Left: Friction fit lid with case splitting artifact and metal handles.

The centering / cutting to width of the three board top/bottom provides two ¼ " lengths for tray rails. In all cases the stock for tops and bottoms was trimmed of tongue and groove material before the centering operations were started. The case parts were cut using the

Taming the ROTOZIP® Spiral Saw

material fence on the WorkBench. The cuts were marked using a framing square and checked against the marks on the perimeter of the depth gauge before the cut was completed. All of the rough cut parts were bundled together, their best edge sanded, and re-cut using a fence and the sanded edge to cut the parts to a standard width in this case a set of eight ends and a set of eight front/back case parts. The resulting cases had consistent dimensions and A L L of the cases were within 14 7/8 - 14 15/ 16 " in their diagonal measurement. The diagonal measurements were not measured during the glueing/clamping process.

One problem occurred, which was not noticed until late. About 8" of a case front was under width, making the top shoulder of its groove too small. It left a gap between the top panel and the edge that filled with urethane glue on the inside and exposed the shoulder of the tongue on the final outer edge. This could have been avoided by cutting the groove for the top further from the edge. The effect of this can be measured, this set of boxes is 7 3/8 " and the original is 7 ¼ " high.

I did some sanding on the B sides of the cedar. If you really are concerned about the condition of the B sides, have them prepared at a cabinet shop by sanding or planing. The planer marks on the B sides appear in depressions and heavy sanding with portable equipment helps but can make the rest of the surface uneven. If the B side's stock condition is unacceptable, sanding with portable equipment may not be acceptable to you. The results, in my case, were smooth interiors, with an occasional planer feed roll mark.

The decorative cut on the bottom used a simple template to guide the ROTOZIP®. The large offset from the pattern is a result of the one inch offset when the depth gauge was used as the guide. No splitting occurred, however this was a very conservative pattern with ample amounts of case in the middle, edges, and only half of the available depth used for the decoration. The template was double face taped to the case and cut clockwise. Note that the template exceeds the length of an end. See Fig. 4-11.

A chuck in a rechargeable screwdriver was used to drill pilot holes for the latches and hinges. The holes were prepared by driving a screw into the holes before a cut off screw was driven into the hole. The screws were cut off using a diagonal cutter at approximately 3/8 " in length. The damaged threads should be removed from the end of the screws so that they follow the threads in the prepared holes. The holes were fortified with glue. The rechargeable screwdriver/chuck provides a light convenient combination for installing hinges and latches. The rechargeable screwdriver/chuck could be a small tool box alternative to a drill, being easy to handle, small, reversible, and usable for drill and screwdriver bits.

The wood latch on the original Bureau Box would occasionally release the pin on the lid. A catch was added to hold the latch on the pin in the lid. The catch was simply a length if tin can edge catching a groove on the lid pin. The catch can be very small using a very shallow kerf cut in the lid pin with a hack saw blade.

by Joel N. Gessele

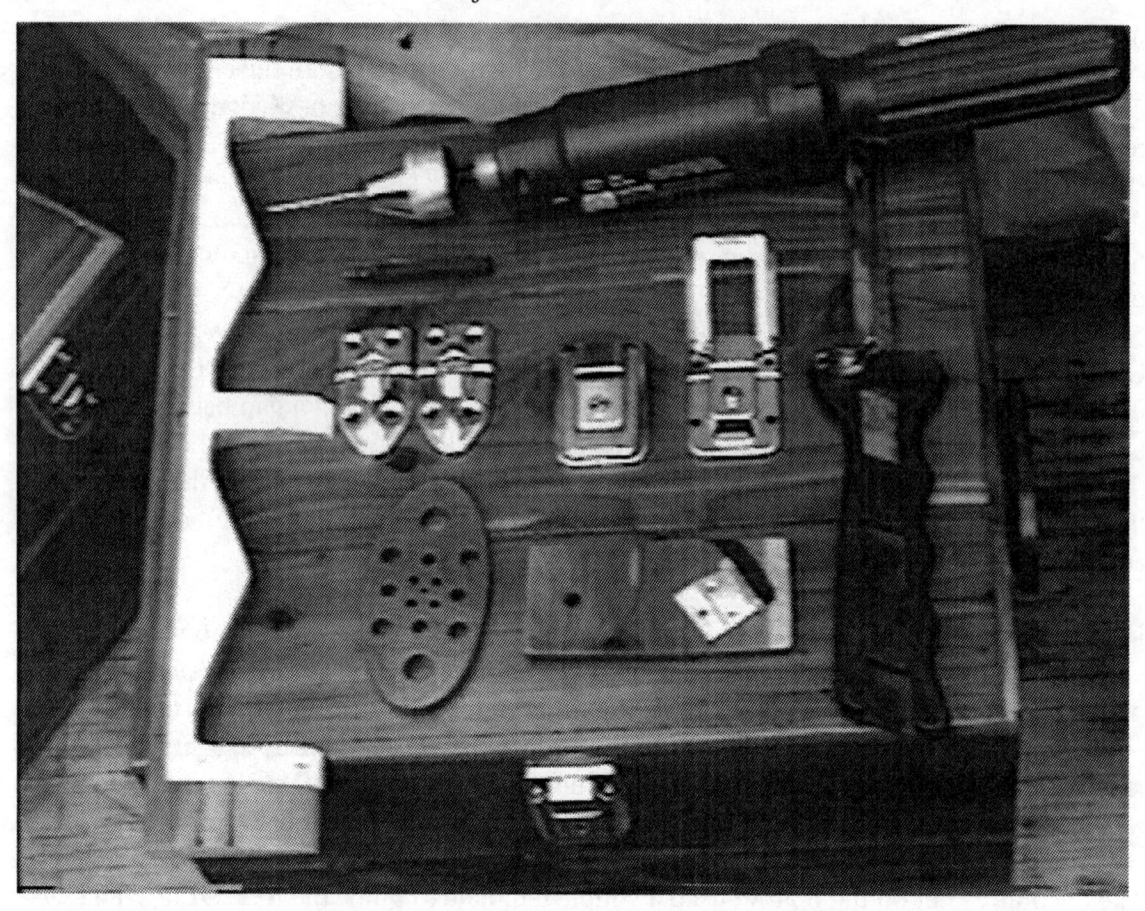

Fig. 4-11: Top: Rechargeable screwdriver with drill chuck and screwdriver bit. Right side: Hack saw Blade and holder used to cut kerf in lid pin. Bottom right: Catch added to a model of the wooden latch, Bottom center: Oval Handle. Left side: Template for decorative bottom cut. Center right: Locking catches open and closed. Center left: Tear Drop hinges.

Taming the ROTOZIP® Spiral Saw

Taming the ROTOZIP® Spiral Saw

Electrical Box Covers:

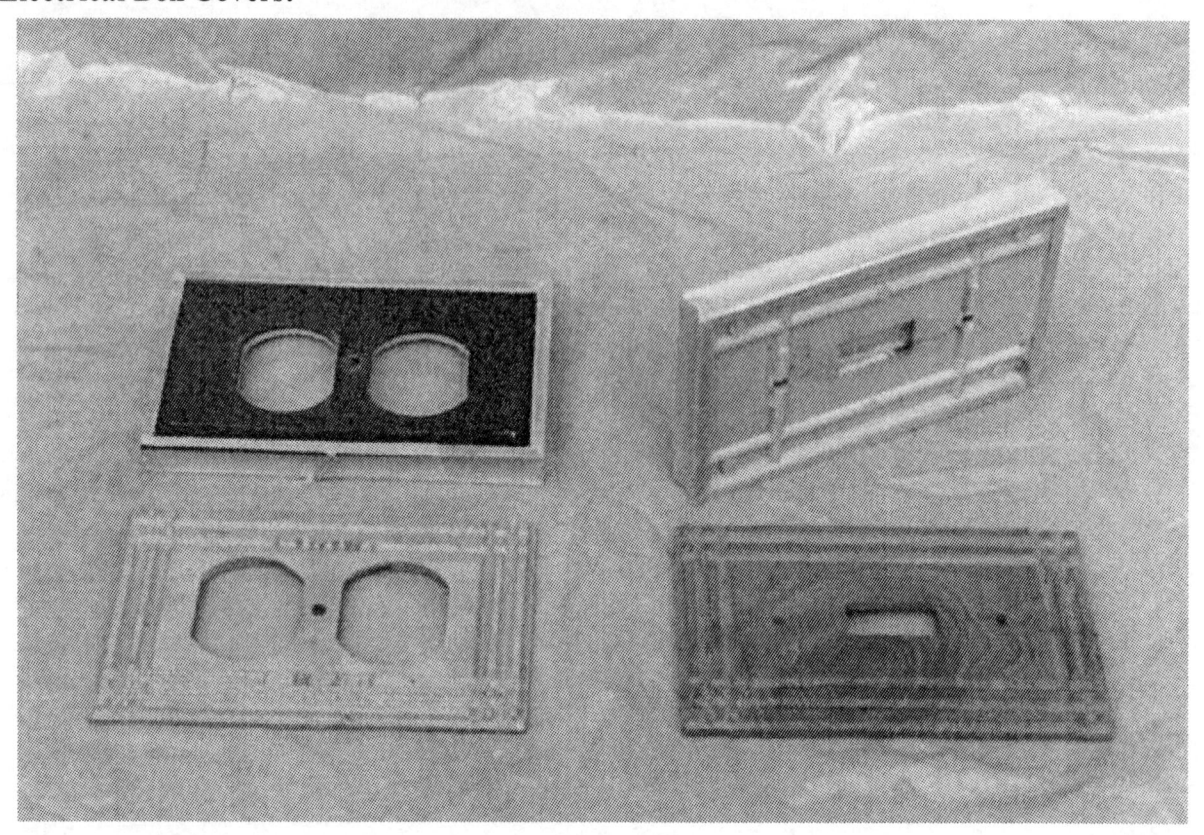

Fig. 5-01: Unfinished Covers with Templates.

Electrical Box cover: Description

The Electrical Box covers complimenting the decor of a room may be the finishing touch in a decorating project or a larger cover may be needed. A different sized custom cover may be desired as a decoration or to protect a larger area around the Electrical Box. The problem is finding appropriate materials and then accurately cutting the material. Since Electrical Box covers are commercially available in a wide variety of materials including ceramics, wood, metal, and plastic, the same materials can be used for custom covers.

Commercial covers are 7/32 " thick around the mounting screw holes and the outer edge. The thickness around the mounting screw supplies strength and stiffness. The additional thickness around the outer edge compensate for Electrical Box irregularities and provides a tight fit against the wall. It would be desirable for the custom covers to inherit these features.

One approach is to use 1/8 " material and make a flat cover. The process outlined here will permit the use of thicker material and allow a tight fit and a minimum investment of time in patterns. Existing covers provide a viable pattern for interior dimensions which will be the same for custom covers. The exterior dimensions can be changed with a fence to offset the cut or a pattern to guide the cut. Totally custom covers can be made by creating a unique shape for a pattern and completing the same steps.

by Joel N. Gessele

Electrical Box cover: Materials:
Cedar, Birch Plywood, Vinyl floor tiles, Pattern Stock (optional, hardboard or actual cover stock).
Crazy Glue

Electrical Box cover: Tools
Commercial Covers to be used as patterns: Outlet cover - Switch box cover
ROTOZIP® bits as needed
Expanded base and portable fence
WorkBench and fence
4" C-Clamps

Electrical Box Cover: Plan
The templates, made from commercial covers, provide a quick accurate pattern for the interior features of the covers. The outline can follow the template or a larger plate made by using the portable fence to offset the cutting from the template. A custom outline can be cut using a custom template.

Electrical Box cover: Blueprint
Commercial Covers are a better source of internal dimensions.

Electrical Box cover: Cutting
1. Tape two covers together, face to face, by putting tape around the edge. After the tape has been applied to the edge press the excess to the back of the covers. If ¾ " tape is used, 1/16 " of tape should be folded on the back surfaces of the covers.

Taming the ROTOZIP® Spiral Saw

Fig. 5-02: Electrical Box Cover Templates. Both templates were used for the samples in this project. The outlet cover shows the effects of exposed flutes on one edge of the template. The tape is removed and a small curl of tape coils off the middle of the template that was in contact with the stock. A dark brown and ivory cover was used for the outlet cover template. Some attention was needed to keep the ROTOZIP® and bit exactly vertical when cutting the internal parts because the backs of the covers do not have a completely flat surface to guide the depth gauge.

2. Clamp the pattern (taped covers) to the material in a position that will allow drilling of the screw holes and cutting of the interior holes.

3. Drill the screw cover hole(s). You can plunge cut the holes with the ROTOZIP®, but drilling is simpler.

by Joel N. Gessele

4. Place a Sabrecut bit or Guidepoint bit in the ROTOZIP® and set the depth gauge to it's minimum extension, exposing the maximum amount of the bits shaft. The non-fluted portion of the shaft will be used as a guide against the pattern. If the covers used for the template are valued, put an extra layer of tape on the template and put a layer of tape on the bit to cover the flutes at the level of the template.

5. Plunge cut the switch hole or the outlet holes that are accessible from the present position. Re-clamp and plunge cut the remaining interior features. Be careful not to reposition the pattern on the material when reclamping. Use a #4-40 x 1" to 1 ½ " bolts to hold the pattern to the material.

6a. If a same sized cover is desired. rout the perimeter using the taped covers as the pattern.

6b. If a larger cover is desired, install the expanded base and a portable fence in the expanded base at the desired offset. Cut the exterior, using the pattern and the fence on the expanded base.

Fig. 5-03: Electrical Box Cover with inner cuts completed and #4 bolt holding the template to the material beneath. Part of the outer perimeter has been cut.

6c. If a custom shape is desired, place the pattern on the material using the screw holes and interior features to register the pattern on the material. Cut the custom contour using the shaft as a guide. If the result desired is only a larger cover, use a portable fence and the expanded base or the depth gauge to offset the bit from the edge of the template.

7a. If ¼ " material is used, obtain the switch or outlets, position them on the back of the cover, and draw an outline around the switch or outlet. Clamp the cover face down and freehand rout the inside of the outline to a depth of 1/8 ". This allows the cover plate to fit against the edges of the electrical box.

Fig. 5-04: Electrical Box Cover with switch placed for outlining. Outline will provide a pattern for freehand routing to inset the switch surface into the switch cover. The cover will then fit close to the wall or on the surface of the electrical box.

7b. If 1/8" material is used. cut an outline base to place under the custom cover. The outline base fills the space under the custom cover and around the box. Glue the outline base to the custom cover yielding a ¼ " edge.

8. On outlet covers, fortify the remaining material in the center with crazy glue. Fortify the screw holes, and the inside of the back top and bottom edges. On Fig. 5-01 a little of the glue has followed the grain and can be seen as darker grain in the unfinished decorative grooves of the outlet plate.

by Joel N. Gessele

9. Change the bit and reposition the fence to customize the cover with:
   - edge roundover
   - edge bevel
   - surface carving

Electrical Box cover: Preparation for Assembly
10. Sand and smooth as appropriate for the material used. A triangular file may be used to square the corners of the slot for the switch. A jewelry file may be needed for smoothing decorative cuts.

11. Prepare the screw holes for the type of screw(s) that will be used to attach the cover to the electrical box, counter sink the hole surface or use decorative round head screw.

Electrical Box cover: Finish
12. Sign and date the back of the plate.

13. Finish to complement decorating suite in a manner compatible with the materials used for the covers.

Electircal Box cover: Results:
This project was a surprise. It took only a few minutes to cut the first outlet cover. The first switch cover had some clamping difficulties but both covers were basically sound.

If the commercial covers used for patterns are needed, protect the pattern with an extra layer of tape. Wrap the bit with tape if the flute is too pronounced at the bottom of the template, but do not withdraw the bit from the collet to expose more of the shaft.

The covers made to demonstrate the procedure are standard sizes. The real usefulness of the procedure is to make non-standard sized covers to solve decorating problems. Large plates to protect wall paint or unusual shapes may be a better application of the procedure.

Taming the ROTOZIP® Spiral Saw
Bracket, Board and Stringer Shelf:

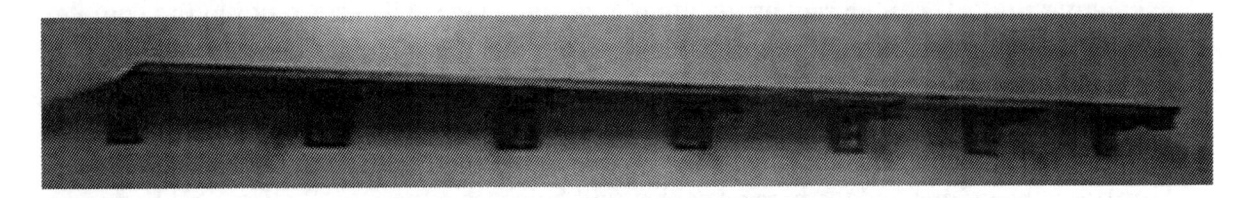

Fig. 6-01: Completed 8 foot version of the Bracket, Board and Stringer Shelf.

Bracket, Board and Stringer shelf: Description

The Bracket, Board and Stringer shelf is a variation of a CD rack from WORKBENCH March-April 2001. The interesting feature of the CD rack was the use of a slot to position book ends along the shelf. The original concept was modified to:
- Minimize the amount of wood used,
- Use readily available materials,
- Maximize the shelf surface,
- Build a shelf that is easy to install, and
- Include the book end feature as independent ends or paired ends with a solid connector.

This project had a terrible start. The template didn't print full size and had to be drawn on the template material, the cut and ask questions later approach ruined a board, burned a router bit, and put a hole in a second board, the solution to these problems was simple, guide the ROTOZIP® by holding the expanded base not the handle or the body of the tool. When the ROTOZIP® is set up with a portable fence, it is easy to overpower the depth gauge adjustment screw and its setting if you attempt to guide the base/fence with the handle or the body of the ROTOZIP®. After this lesson was relearned, I was able to complete eight feet of groove and 24 feet of rabbeting without loosing the settings or burning the bit as the depth serendipitously increased and bottomed out. The depth gauge is easily overpowered, it cannot be tightened enough to allow control to be passed through it, therefore the forces on it must be minimized. Make the adjustments, test cut, and story board cut, then visually check the depth gauge and make sure that it is tight. Proceed by guiding the ROTOZIP® holding the Expanded Base. Usually the spline and point of the expanded base provide a sufficient area to safely guide the ROTOZIP® in the expanded base.

Always check at least one dimension on printouts that are to be used as patterns to assure yourself that a fit to page option was not used or that your printer did not compress the image. The template displays at the correct dimension when displayed on the screen, but both the dot matrix printer and the Digital Service at OFFICE DEPOT prints a template that is too small when the dimensions on the printing are re-measured.

by Joel N. Gessele

The stringers are oriented to make maximum use of the material for strength and provide additional strength by butting it against the bracket. The stringer is cut using a template to assist in cutting a right angle end and a decorative notch in the stringer. In addition to a decorative stringer, configurations that didn't consume the shelf surface or require complex joinery were pursued. A shelf supported underneath met these requirements, providing that the back/upper corner is strong enough to resist the rotation force of the loaded shelf. The direction of the wood grain for the bracket must be vertical to use as many growth rings as practical in the tenon. This may make the groove in the shelf bottom as the weakest link. Fortifying the groove and the bracket rabbet will help strengthen the shelf and still provide the widest possible shelf from the materials (See Fig. 6-02). Two actions were taken to strengthen the shelf, screws into the edge of the shelf board and gluing bracket/stringer/board. The use of connected bookends, or lengths of middle board will fill the middle slot when a continuous shelf surface is needed and wood usage is not a concern.

This project uses common lumber and exploits the ROTOZIP® close to its maximum cutting depth of one inch. The decorative cut and the cross cutting of stringers are an opportunity to use the ROTOZIP® on more substantial stock. This project uses a template to cut a square end on the stringer and cut a series of similar parts.

This version leaves the screws exposed making the assembly is simple and requires few clamps. If the appearance of the shelf is to be improved, replace the screws with dowels/glue, clamping during assembly, and quality hardwood. The endcaps are shown on the test shelf and are included to cover the shelf board end grain. The ends of the stringers are 3/4 " back from the edge, it would be easy to wrap the shelf with a wood strip to make the shelf appear 2 1/4 " thick.

Originally, the brackets were to be mounted to the wall and the shelf laid in place. This did not appear to build a strong shelf and irregularities in the wall surface did not make it easy to install the shelf. Pre assembling the Bracket/Stringer/Board, makes a strong shelf and simplifies the assembly at the expense of installation ease. The difficulty during installation is driving the upper screw through the bracket. A long driver bit helps, but a lot of force is needed to drive the drywall screws.

Taming the ROTOZIP® Spiral Saw

Upper: Side View of Back of Test Shelf.
Middle: Side view of Front of Test Shelf.
Bottom: Front view of Test Shelf, with four Book Ends, Endcaps, 33 1/2 inches long.

Fig. 6-02: Test Shelf (finished) Views

by Joel N. Gessele

Bracket, Board and Stringer shelf: Materials for 8 foot Shelf

2- 1" x 4" x 8' (3/4" x 3 ½ " x 8 ') # 2 common or length to fit your requirements for main shelf.
1- 1" x 4" x 8' (3/4" x 3 ½ " x 8 ') # 2 common or length to fit your requirements for center or book end connectors
1- 1" x 2" x 8' (3/4" x 1 ½ " x 8 ') # 2 common or length to fit your requirements for stringers and end caps (7 stringers and 2 endcaps for an eight foot shelf.)
1- 1" x 4" x 3' (3/4" x 3 ½ " x 8 ') # 2 common or length to fit your requirements for brackets (7 brackets for 8' shelf).
49- 1 ¼ " Drywall screws to attach bracket to stringer, shelf to stringers. endcaps to stringers, shelf to bracket, and to strengthen the edge of the back shelf board.
14-2 ½ " Drywall screws to attach brackets to wall.
Glue, Stain, Shellac, Alcohol, Sandpaper

The test shelf was made with 33 1/2 long shelf boards to span three 16 " on center wall studs.. Since the wood was inexpensive, a solid center connector was made as the middle shelf board and connector for the book ends.

Bracket, Board and Stringer shelf: Tools

1/4" straight cut router bit, Chamfer bit,
Guide point bit or Sabrecut bit for cross cutting and trimming
Framing square or WorkBench (see Appendix)
Circle cutter attachment and Expanded Base (see Appendix), Fence for use with Expanded Base
Drill, 3/16" bit for drywall screw holes in brackets, Phillips screwdriver bit
C-clamps
Electric Sander.
Framing Square

Bracket, Board and Stringer shelf: Plan

The shelf dimensioned here is 8 feet long, 10 inches wide, and has seven stringers on 16 " centers. The length and number of stringers can be adjusted to match your requirements. If the book end featured is not desired, a 10 ½ shelf can be made with three boards. Endcaps can be made to cover the end grain of the shelf boards.

This project uses a fence attached to Expanded Base to cut grooves and dadoes and a template to cut stringers. The first activity is to make the template and allow the glue dry. The second activity is to prepare the shelf boards, followed by cutting the stringers using the template. A dry assembly is used to prepare the parts for gluing and final assembly by drilling holes for the screws to accurately position the parts on final assembly with urethane glue. The parts are sanded, conditioned, and stained prior to final assembly.
1. Make Template for stringers.

2. Cut Grooves and rabbets in shelf material.
3. Cut stringers, brackets, and end caps.
4. Bevel edges on stringers, brackets, and book ends.
5. Story board the shelf in its position on the wall using tape to mark positions of the studs and transfer the tape to a story board. Drill holes in shelf boards for attaching the stringers and bookends.
6. Sand all components.
7. Treat all components with sanding sealer, stain all components.
8. Attach stringers, brackets, and back shelf board with screws and glue.
9. Attach front shelf board to stringer subassembly with screws and glue.
10. Finish and install.

Bracket, Board and Stringer shelf: Blueprint

Fig. 6-03: Component Dimensions.

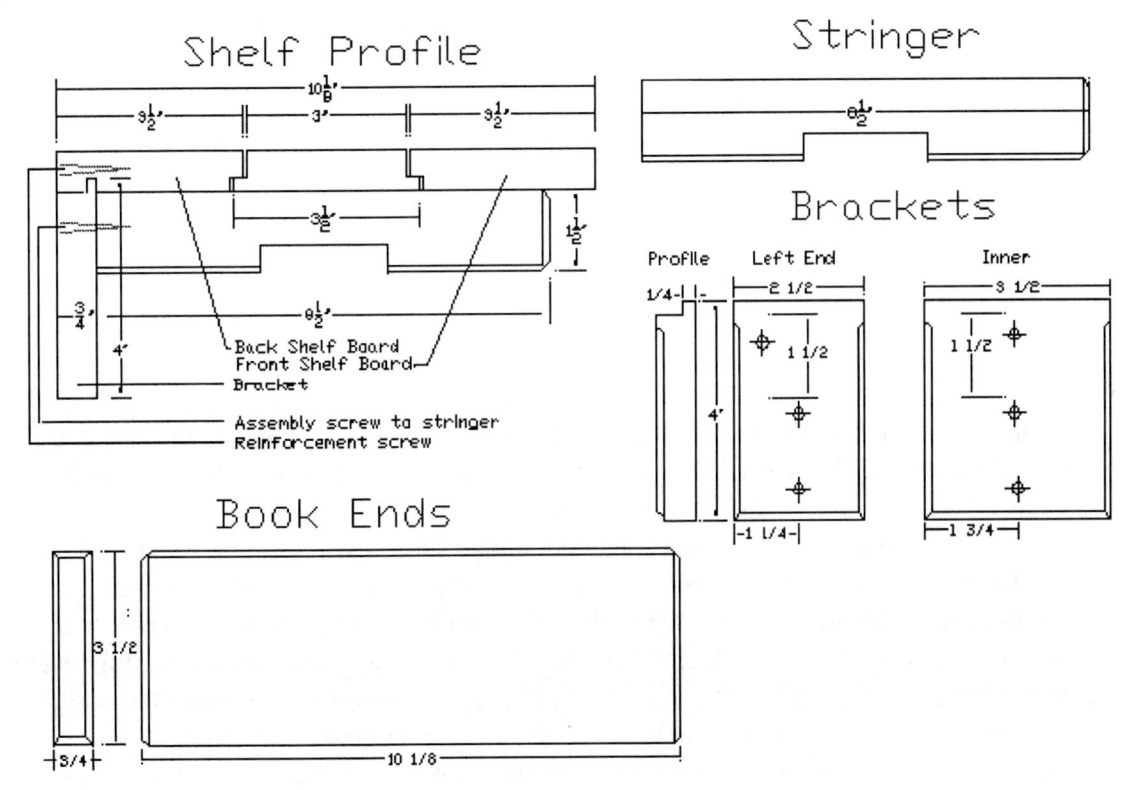

Bracket, Board and Stringer shelf: Cutting

1. Prepare the template material by laying out the dimensions on the material selected for the template. The stringer cut by the template is set back from the shelf's front edge to minimize the stringer's exposure. The notch cut in the stringer is decorative and it was kept small, variations could be more elaborate without compromising the strength of the shelf. The framing square was used to guide the ROTOZIP® by clamping the square to the template material. The template was smoothed using a rasp and sandpaper before

by Joel N. Gessele

the 1 x 2 was attached to the back of the template. Allowing the 1 x 2 to extend beyond the edge of the template provides a tool rest to launch the cross cuts. The edges of the template were fortified with a coating of glue to stabilize the particle board.

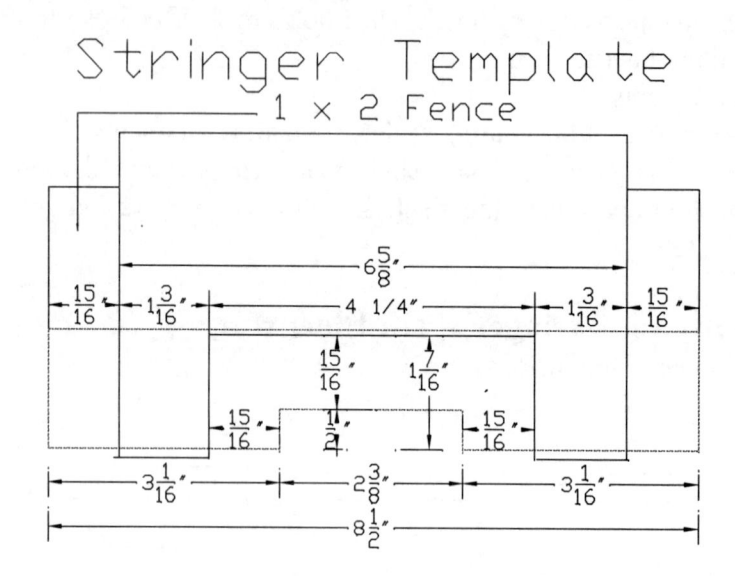

Stringer Template

1 x 2 Fence

Dimensions: $6\frac{5}{8}"$, $\frac{15}{16}"$, $1\frac{3}{16}"$, $4\ 1/4"$, $1\frac{3}{16}"$, $\frac{15}{16}"$, $\frac{15}{16}"$, $1\frac{7}{16}"$, $\frac{15}{16}"$, $\frac{1}{2}"$, $\frac{15}{16}"$, $3\frac{1}{16}"$, $2\frac{3}{8}"$, $3\frac{1}{16}"$, $8\frac{1}{2}"$

2. The groove for the brackets is the first item to be cut. Its position is determined by the width if the bracket material. Test cut scrap material to set the Expanded Base and fine tune the settings. When set, tighten the Expanded Base and the Depth gauge. DO NOT CONTROL THE ROTOZIP® BY HOLDING THE HANDLE OF THE ROTOZIP® OR THE BODY, you will overpower the depth gauge set screw. Hold the Expanded Base, minimize the pressure on the depth gauge, and keep the power cord away from the depth gauge. The portable fence should be ¾ " thick to allow the fence to ride in the uncut edge when the center shelf board rabbet is cut. One groove and four rabbets are needed. See results for variations that may change the amount of routing applied to your project. Two methods were used for the groove, continuos or stopped. A continuos groove was used on the 8 foot shelf. Stopped grooves were used on the test shelf. Stopped grooves are ideal if you prepare a story board locating the positions for the brackets. Cut stopped grooves using the story board for the wall studs. Begin the cut in the middle, by tilting the base on its side with the fence against the edge of the board. Use the center mark on the circle cutter to estimate the progress of the cut.

Taming the ROTOZIP® Spiral Saw

Fig. 6-05: Dimension check and Expanded Base setup. Check position of groove to make sure it is inset the width of the bracket stock from the back edge. Check the front edge inset to equal to width of stringer stock. Check length of stringer. Upper: Fence is 5/8 " thick particle board scrap with two #2 machine screws and burrs. Two holes in expanded base fence are adequate, rather than the six shown here.

3. Position the material to make the stringers by holding the template over the material and screwing dry wall screws through the template into the stringer material. Check template to assure that the stringer is drawn tightly to the template. Screw the material and template into scrap board clamped to a stable base. Cut the required number of stringers, seven for an 8 foot long shelf. Cut two end caps by cutting the notch and then moving its position in the template or adding a 3/4" spacer to offset the cut to yield the longer stringers used for the end caps.

by Joel N. Gessele

Fig. 6-06: Template loaded with 1 x 2 stock in position for attachment to board clamped to WorkBench. Black drywall screws to hold 1 x 2 stock to fence are visible at center and lower corner of fence. Completed stringers and endcaps on right. Endcaps must be 3/4 " longer at both ends, not 3/4 " long at one end as pictured.

4. Cut book ends if desired.
   Cut brackets, drill holes in brackets, bevel edges, sand all components.

Bracket, Board and Stringer shelf: Preparation for Assembly
5. Fortify back shelf board with screws into the back edge. Sand shelves.
6. Treat components with wood conditioner and stain components.
7. Drill holes in the shelf boards at 16 " centers or at positions where the wall studs are located for your installation according to the story board.

Bracket, Board and Stringer shelf: Assembly

8. Begin assembly by placing bracket in groove of a back shelf board and securing the bracket and stringer at right angles to the side and edge of the board. Attach the stringer to the back shelf board with screws and glue.

Fig. 6-06: Dry assembly and brackets (2 sizes). First step is 90 degree joining of bracket to stringer. Next step is joining stringer to back shelf board. Check board to bracket and shelf board edge to stringer length to make sure they are 90 degree angles in both planes.

9. Repeat the assembly steps for the remaining brackets and stringers.
10. Position the front shelf board on the back shelf board/stringer/bracket assembly and attach with screws and glue. If a removable or connected book shelf segment is planned, use them to space the back and front shelf boards and use a sheet of paper to provide additional clearance. If a strip along the front of the shelf is to be added, check

by Joel N. Gessele

to assure alignment with front edge. Caution: Check progress to assure that the assembly is straight and not twisted.

Bracket, Board and Stringer shelf: Finish

11. Shelf has many parts and staining was suggested before starting assembly to simplify staining process. Finish as desired.

Bracket, Board and Stringer shelf: Results

Shelf width in Blueprints is 10 1/8 " wide. Actual shelf was 10 1/8" from wall but width of shelf boards including gaps was +9 7/8". Boards used were under 3 1/2". Shelf boards plus stringers assembly developed a twist during assembly. Weakest point was from corner of back shelf groove to top of shelf. Fortify this area by drilling starter holes and driving screws into the back edge. Gluing bracket/stringers/boards increases shelf strength substantially.

This project had the long 1/4" grooves made with the portable fence. The first attempt to make the grooves ruined the board when the depth gauge screw was overpowered and the depth of the groove increased. Prevent this problem by controlling the ROTOZIP® and expanded base by holding the expanded base. This solution works well but was not immediately obvious.

Driving screws through the bracket into the end grain of the stringer was necessary to simplify construction. It was not practical to place the brackets on the wall before positioning a shelf/stringer assembly. Some difficulty was experienced driving the screws through the bracket into the wall stud. Problem was mainly the angle and power needed to drive the dry wall screws. A long driver bit for the drywall screws would be useful during the installation. The shelf must be level and supported as a unit for installation.

The resulting shelf met the material use requirements, it is strong, doesn't tilt, the full width is available, and shows some decorative elements. The twist did not disappear on installation or loading. Check your assembly to make sure that you make a flat straight shelf assembly. Simple beveled rectangles were used for brackets, a more decorative shape for the bracket and stringer is possible.

The ripping of the end brackets to the 2 1/2 " width using the ROTOZIP® and the WorkBench yielded angled edges. Re-cutting did not remove the angle and made a double bevel.

The rabbeting of the brackets used the maximum cutting depth of the 1/4 " straight cut bit as did the center board rabbeting. If you want to reduce the amount of routing, consider

Taming the ROTOZIP® Spiral Saw

making stopped grooves for the brackets (test shelf) and short lengths for the book end positioners.

Beveling the brackets and stringers was a compromise for depth and exposure in setting up the chamfer bit. Avoid contact with the circle cutter round adapter by the bottom of the chamfer bit. Setting up the Chamfer bit required setting up the expanded base and inserting the bit through the assembly.

A test shelf was built to demonstrate the suggestions and process improvements learned from the original 8 foot shelf. The shelf was made smaller to allow greater detail in illustrations and to test the strength of the shelf. The strength is a related to the length of the tenon in the back shelf board. The strongest shelf would be a continuous "bracket". A continuous bracket would support the shelf board but use too much wood. The length of tenon used in the test shelf is 2 1/4 + 3 1/4 + 2 1/4, the width of the brackets and the groove in the back shelf board.

Fig. 6-06: Test shelf prior to assembly. Left Front: End cap laid down sideways to final assembly position. Left Center: Bottom of shelf with end bracket in position and inner bracket on side to show tenon on bracket and stopped groove in back shelf board. Bracket to stringer screw is exposed at back of bracket. Tenon and groove were not stained to encourage glue adsorption and make a stronger joint. Right: Complete assembly with bookends placed in position without middle board. Middle board was removed to prevent it from being glued in place.

by Joel N. Gessele

The test shelf was loaded with 40 pounds of text books, equal to 32 inches of large textbooks that filled a medium sized moving box. The shelf was mounted with six drywall screws through the brackets for the test. The books were loaded and the structure observed. There was no deformation of the shelf or brackets, the joints did not break their glue bonds, and the brackets did not split. More weight was added with a pull on the shelf to see if additional weight could be borne by the test shelf. It was difficult to drive the fastening screws through the brackets into the test support and withdraw the screws from the test support.

by Joel N. Gessele

Computer Table:

Fig. 7-01: Computer Tables profile showing hand hold in sides of case. Hand holds in the case sides and back serve as electrical cord access.

Computer Table: Description

The Computer Table uses 3/8 " thick strawboard, the material was chosen for its novelty and a thickness that provides 1/4" tenons by removing only 1/8" of material. The configuration and rough dimensions is controlled by the average computer keyboard width of 20 1/2" and keyboard working height of 28". The Computer Table can be configured to hold CPU, printer, and Monitor. A table and accessories can be made from one 4' x 8' sheet of material and 26 feet of 1 x 2 (3/4" x 1 1/2") molding. Two Tables were made to allow the monitor to be placed on one, lightening the table, making it easier to move within the tethering limits of the power and video cable. A second table is needed as the base for the second monitor on dual display systems.

Stacking shelves were built to allow the space to be configured as needed. The stackers used full and partial tops to allow printers to be place on the shelves and paper routed to the printer. Full width shelves were made to discourage items from falling down along the edges. The back has at least a 3/4" clearance for routing cables.

Taming the ROTOZIP® Spiral Saw

The keyboard tray is adjustable and will fit flush with the front. The preferred position is with 10" extended. The interior of the tray is accessible from the front and can store paper or manuals. The keyboard tray has a 3/8" lip to hold the keyboard and provide a grip.

The tables were prototyped with Strawboard to confirm measurements and test construction techniques with Strawboard (particle board). Another reason to use the straw board was to exploit an environmentally friendly material. The corners were fortified with urethane glue to prevent the anticipated disfigurement at corners. The internal skeleton was added to strengthen, the table and provide a structure to support the keyboard tray. The internal skeleton provides additional material for the fasteners for the casters. The screws attaching the casters bridge two skeleton members, two screws in a side skeleton member and two screws in a front/back member at each caster plate.

All case parts are 21 1/4 " wide using most of two 8 ' strips cut from a 4 x 8 sheet. The tray parts and stacker tops can also be cut from the strips. The case parts were cut from the strips cut at Home Depot on their panel saw, making it easy to handle and haul the material. Trimming and cutting the smaller parts was done with the ROTOZIP® and WorkBench. The 21 inch width of the keyboard tray top is very close to the width limit for ripping panels on the WorkBench.

The strawboard is also being tested as a chair mat to replace a plastic one that developed cracks. Two chair mats were made from a 4 x 8 sheet where the corners were rounded and surfaces painted.

by Joel N. Gessele

Fig. 7-02: Completed Computer Tables with keyboard trays extended and stackers. Both tables have two stackers, two large on the right, one large and one small on the left. The keyboard trays are extended.

Computer Table: Materials for 8 foot Shelf

2- 21 1/4" x 29" x 3/8" (Sides) Strawboard, Plywood, or MDF for case sides.
1- 21 1/4" x 29" x 3/8" (Back) Strawboard, Plywood, or MDF for case back.
2- 21 1/4" x 21" x 3/8" (Top/Bottom) Strawboard, Plywood, or MDF for top and bottom panels.
1- 20 3/4" x 19 1/4" x 3/8" (Tray Top) Strawboard, Plywood, or MDF for top and bottom panels.
1- 20 "   x 19 1/2" x 3/8" (Tray Bottom) Strawboard, Plywood, or MDF for top and bottom panels.
4- 1" x 2" x24" (3/4" x 1 ½ " x 24") # 2 common or Hemlock for vertical tray supports
2- 1" x 2" x21" (3/4" x 1 ½ " x 21") # 2 common or Hemlock for bottom front and back.
2- 1" x 2" x18" (3/4" x 1 ½ " x 18 1/8") # 2 common or Hemlock for bottom sides
2- 1" x 2" x20 1/4" (3/4" x 1 ½ " x 20 1/4") # 2 common or Hemlock for tray rails.
2- 1" x 2" x20 1/4" (3/4" x 1 ½ " x 19 1/4") # 2 common or Hemlock for tray spacers.
1- 1" x 2" x20 7/8" (3/4" x 1 ½ " x 20 7/8") # 2 common or Hemlock for tray front.
X- 21   x XX" x 3/8' (Stacker Top) Strawboard, Plywood, or MDF for Shelf panels.
2X- 5 3/8" x 18 1/2" x 3/8' (Stacker Riser) Strawboard, Plywood, or MDF for Shelf risers.
----X --- Variable, depends on the materials that remain, shelves were made with gaps between sections where equipment or books would bridge the gap.

Urethane Glue, Shellac, Alcohol, Sandpaper, Enamel,

Computer Table: Tools

1/4" straight cut router bit,
Guide point bit or Sabrecut bit for cross cutting and trimming
Guide point bit for trimming
Framing square or WorkBench (see Appendix)
Circle cutter attachment and Expanded Base (see Appendix), Fence for use with Expanded Base
Drill, 3/16" bit for drywall screw holes in brackets, Phillips screwdriver bit
hacksaw blade-handle
6" rasp
C-clamps
Electric Sander.
Framing Square
Bar Clamps and or twine to make twist clamps.
Template for 1 x 2 right angle cuts, framing square and C Clamps, or radial arm saw.

Computer Table: Plan

A simple overview of this project is in order before you dive into the drawings and instructions. The case is simply two sides with a "U" shaped dado on the three inside edges. The top/back/bottom have rabbets to go into the side pieces. The top and bottom use the same rabbet fitted into a dado on the inside of the back. The 1 x 2 's are placed to provide a skeleton to aid in assembly, provide a tray rail, and strengthen the case.

by Joel N. Gessele

Fig. 7-03: Parts, with skeleton members attached, ready for assembly. Bottom: Bottom with perimeter skeleton members. Middle: Side, Back, side case members with skeleton members attached. Top: Top - no skeleton members, inside view -- rabbets are on face.

The 1 x 2 (3/4" x 1 1/2") skeleton can be installed in an assembled case or attached to the individual parts and used to assemble the case. Assembling the case, then installing the skeleton makes a neater skeleton, but more bar clamps are needed. Gluing the support members to the panels allows easy access for clamping and joining the skeleton. The attached skeleton and drywall screws were used to clamp the parts during assembly as the alternate method for assembling the case.

The case shown in the above illustration has the skeleton attached to the individual case parts. The other case was assembled and the skeleton added into the case. The difference between the methods is that more bar clamps are required to assemble the case without the skeleton attached. Attaching the skeleton requires careful positioning of the skeleton members. The case that had the skeleton added after assembly resulted in a neater assembly and the case with the skeleton attached needed to have two vertical supports trimmed.

Computer Table: Blueprint

Taming the ROTOZIP® Spiral Saw

Fig. 7-04: Component Dimensions.

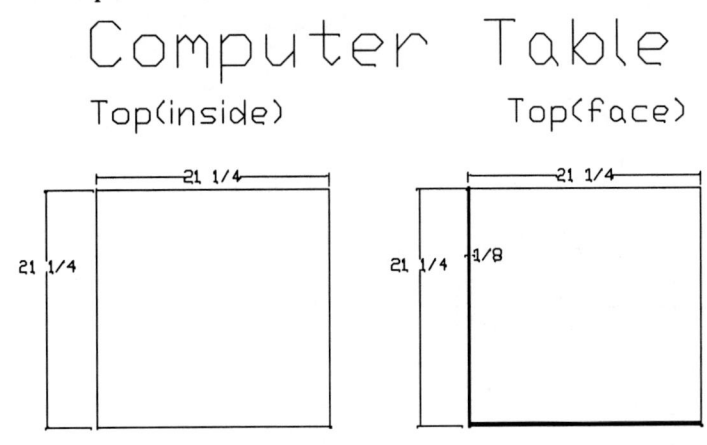

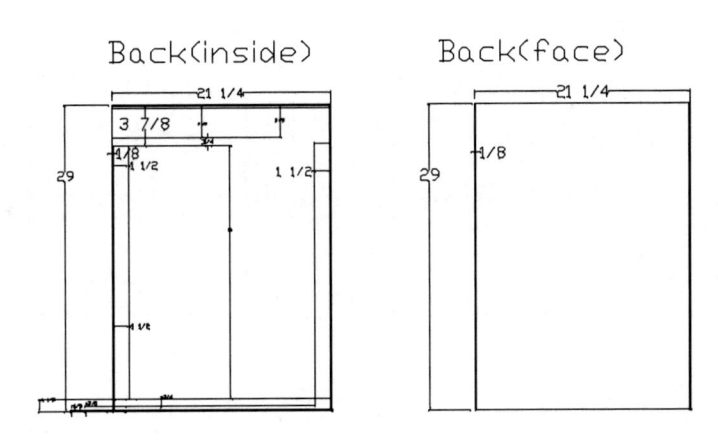

Computer Table

Top(inside) Top(face)

21 1/4   21 1/4
21 1/4   21 1/4   1/8

Back(inside) Back(face)

21 1/4   21 1/4
3 7/8
1/8
1 1/2   1/8
29   29
1 1/2

1 1/2

91

by Joel N. Gessele

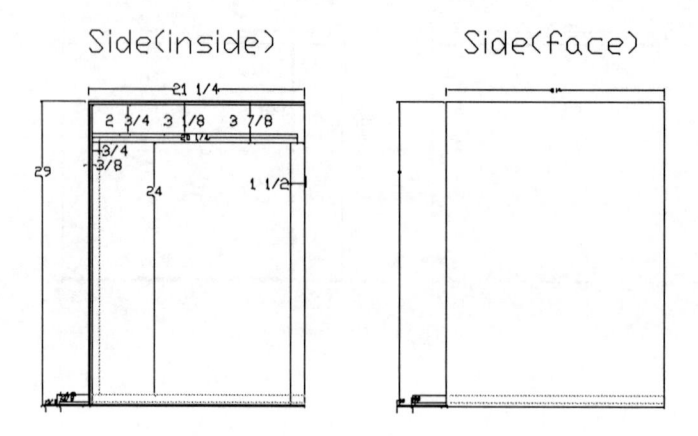

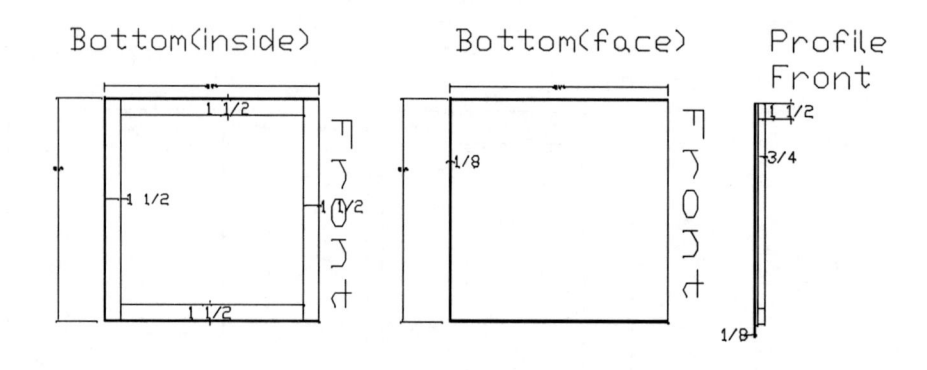

Taming the ROTOZIP® Spiral Saw

Large Stacker

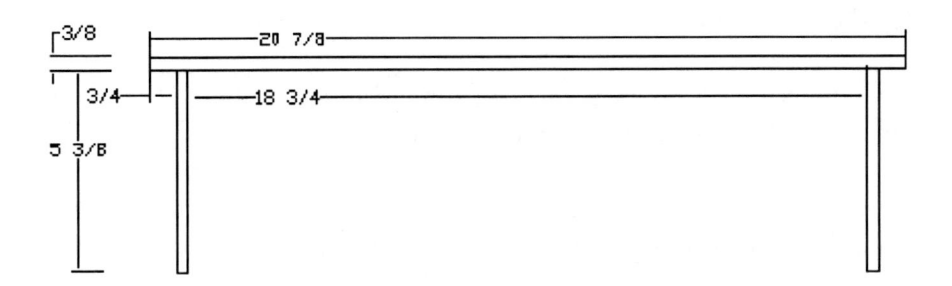

Computer Table: Cutting

1. Cut the 4' x 8' panel into two 21 1/4" x 8 foot x 3/8" strips. Cut three 29 " x 21 1/4 "x 3/8" panels for sides and back. Cut two 21" x 21 1/4" x 3/8" panels for the top and bottom. These are the main 21 1/4" panels and were cut on the panel saw.

Fig. 7-05: Computer Table Parts on 4 x 8 sheet stock. Request two 21 ¼ x 96 panels to be cut at the building supply center. Then have the strips cut into manageable pieces.

by Joel N. Gessele

Expect that the ends of the 21 ¼ cuts will slump on the panel saw and use these for the stacker tops.

2. Cut 21" x 19 7/8" x 3/8" Keyboard tray top. Cut a 19 1/2" x 19 1/4" x 3/8" Tray bottom.
3. Cut four stacker risers 5 3/8 x 18 1/2" x 3/8". Stacker top panels can be varied in depth to allow paper to pass through to a printer from a lower level making the critical dimension the 21" width.

If the above items are cut on the panel saw at the Building Supply Center, the parts and remaining materials are small enough to carry in a car.

4. Cut four 24" vertical supports from 1 x 2 stock. The WorkBench, the template from the Bracket, Board, and Stringer, or a Framing Square can be used to make square cuts. A radial arm saw was used to expedite the skeleton members (see results for explanation).
5. Cut two 1x 2 x 21" Front/back bottom skeleton members, two 1 x 2 x 18 1/8 " side bottom skeleton members.
6. Cut two 1 x 2 x 20 1/4" tray slides and two 1 x 2 x 20" tray spacers, if practical cut them from the same stock.
7. Cut 1/4" x 1/8" stopped dadoes around three edges of the side panels. These panels are non-directional, if you want your panels to be oriented in a particular orientation be sure that the dadoes are on the right edges. Stopped dadoes are used to strengthen the corners. The ideal shoulder is 1/8" thick, a thicker shoulder will add strength needed during assembly. The shoulder was fortified with glue because the panels may break the shoulder during assembly, especially if the panels are bowed. The portable fence and a 1/4" straight cut router bit was used to cut the dado.
8. Cut 1/4 x 1/8" dadoes on the inside back to receive the top/bottom panel rabbets. Check to assure that these rabbets align with the dados of the sides.
9. Cut 1/8" x 1/8" rabbets in the outside back (vertical), outside bottom (3 sides), outside top (3 sides). Two rabbets are needed on the back, three on both the top/bottom panels. The expanded base and WorkBench were used to cut the rabbets. Cut greater than 1/8" rabbets if assembly problems are anticipated and a less than 1/4" tenon is desired to slide into the stopped dadoes.
10. Cut the end of the rabbet off the front of the top/bottom to fit the stopped dadoes. The hacksaw blade-handle using the rabbet as a guide made this process simple and quick, especially on strawboard.

Fig. 7-06: Computer Tables top, with rabbet removed, lower corners, on front edge. Rabbet on three sides is not visible because the inner surface of the top is displayed.

Computer Table: Preparation for Assembly

11. If the stopped dadoes haven't been fortified, fortifiy the shoulder with a thin coat of glue.
12. Check alignment of stopped dadoes between side and back panels. Correct by enlarging the dadoes or making the rabbets deeper (tenon smaller).

    The remaining instructions assume that you have elected to use the internal skeleton to assist in assembly.

13. Glue the skeleton to the inside of the bottom panel. The front is flush, the back and sides are inset 1/8", equal to the rabbets on the face.

by Joel N. Gessele

Fig. 7-07: Computer Tables Bottom, inside- with front at the bottom.

14. The back needs two vertical supports. The vertical offsets are 1/8" from the edge and 1 1/8 (3/8 + 3/4) from the bottom. The dadoes for the top/bottom are visible on the inside of the panel, the 1/8 x 1/8" rabbet is on the vertical face panel sides and are not visible.

Fig. 7-08: Computer Tables back - inside. Dado for top and bottom is visible. Edge inset is not visible.

15. The side panels receive a flush front vertical support and a tray rail. The vertical support is 1 1/8 (3/8 + 3/4) from the bottom and flush with the front edge. The tray support contacts the vertical support 3/4 " from the front edge and even with the edge of the dado in back.

by Joel N. Gessele

Fig. 7-09: Computer Tables Sides with front and tray rail in place. Stopped dado visible at top, back edge, and bottom.

16. If all skeleton members are correctly placed, the bottom and back members can be used hold the side panel in place during gluing with drywall screws. After the assembly is complete and the glue is dry, the screws can be withdrawn and the holes filled with glue and sawdust.
17. Check alignment of dadoes and the keyboard tray rail on the sides with the vertical supports of the back.

Computer Table: Assembly

18. Preferred assembly is the bottom to the back and a side. Urethane glue was used and placed in thin beads on the dado, on the shoulder of the dado, in the corner of the rabbet, and on the end of the tenon. Where needed drywall screws were used to pull and hold the panels together. Bar clamps, if available, are useful to press joints together.
19. After the glue has set, add the other side. Glue, screw, and clamp as needed.
20. Without the top, the keyboard tray can be put in place and assembly started. This step is to start the assembly and prepare the keyboard tray for painting. Place the top in place

and center it. Put the spacers in place and the tray bottom. Adjust the components so that they are centered. Use a 1 x 2 scrap to align the bottom tray at the correct spacing from the sides. Use a scrap panel and blocking to adjust the height of the components. Move the spacers in position by reaching around the back. When all components are in place, clamp the tray top, spacers and bottom. Drill 1/4" holes, through the tray bottom, spacers and into the tray top. The holes will be used for dowels to aid in the partial assembly of the tray so that it can be machined for access and the inside painted. A drill stop was used and the holes in the tray top deepened. The top keyboard panel, spacers, and keyboard tray front were glued, weighted, and clamped. The bottom was not attached to allow access for painting and cutting part of the front to allow use of the inside of the tray for storage.
21. Install the table top in the case, glue and clamp as needed.
22. The tray stackers have the risers inset 3/4 of an inch. from the edge. This allows the stacker to be moved inside the case at an angle and rotated to horizontal. The 3/4" inset provides enough clearance if the risers are only 5 3/8" high. A butt joint is sufficiently strong if it is well made. The full panel stacker is the most difficult to make because it bows up away from the risers. 1 x 2 blocking can be added if needed to strengthen or brace the stackers.
23. Cut a notch in the tray front using a guidepoint bit and the bottom of the keyboard tray top as the guide.

Computer Table: Finish

24. Prepare edges using the ROTOZIP© to trim excess board and glue from the edges using the face of the panels to guide the guide point bit. Use light pressure to avoid rounding the corner or burning the panel face with the guidepoint.
25. Fortify the corners with a coating of glue.
26. Smooth edges using the 6" rasp.
27. Fill voids with glue/sawdust.
28. Cut handhold holes using the template. Template can be printed from the Appendix. The 1 inch width is adequate for molded electrical plugs. Placement is at least the thickness of the keyboard tray bottom below the tray rail. The hand holds were so useful, they were placed in upper and lower levels, a total of 6 handholds, thinking that the lower set could be used for power strip access to the wall outlet.

by Joel N. Gessele

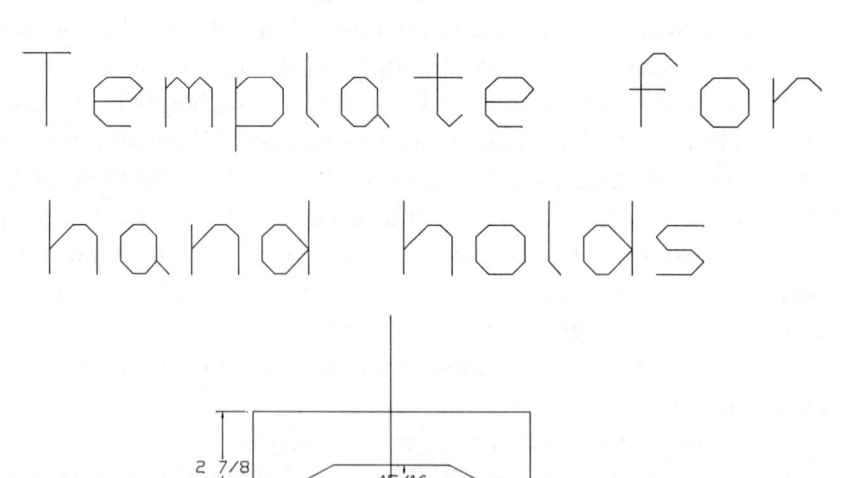

Template for hand holds

Fig. 7-10: Computer Table Hand hold Template. Cut outer oval, smooth edge and allow the edge of the ROTOZIP® depth gauge to cutout creating the one inch wide handhold. Round the edges of the holes with a round over bit. Six handhols were placed in the case; three six inches from the bottom and three below the bottom of the keyboard tray. Two handholds per panel really made handling the table easier.

29. Sand surfaces.
30. Seal the surfaces. The sealer of choice is shellac. Shellac dries fast and will permit either latex or oil based paint to cover the strawboard. Approximately a pint of shellac, diluted 1 : 1 with alcohol. was needed to cover the stackers, keyboard tray, and cases for two tables.
31. Paint. One quart was needed for two coats on the interior, keyboard tray, and four stackers. Three fourths of a quart was used to apply three coats on the exterior of cases of two tables.

Computer Table: Results

The computer table is the largest project attempted with a small set of tools and the ROTOZIP®. Ripping the 4 x 8 panels and having the case, top/bottom, and stacker parts cut on the panel saw at the building supply store makes the project manageable and allows the parts to be taken home without a truck.

The dadoes in the side panels permit the back and top/bottom to be positioned more securely than if two rabbet joints were used. The main problem is that the panels may be or become bowed. Check the storage of the materials to see that is stored on a straight shelf. The width of the dado is the 1/4" straight cut router bit. Cutting the rabbet on the

Taming the ROTOZIP® Spiral Saw

back/top/bottom panels deeper than 1/8" makes assembly easier. The shoulder of the dado is the weakest point and may blow out even if fortified with glue. Making the shoulder of the dado thicker can help prevent the shoulder from shearing off during assembly but the excess must be trimmed to make a square corner.

The keyboard tray appeared to have sufficient clearances, but the paint filled the space making the tray slide with difficulty. The tray bottom was not glued to the tray front and spacers until after the surfaces were painted to avoid this problem. The tray edges and tray support were lubricated to ease movement after the paint was dry. A better approach would be to add a cardboard shim along the length of the spacer. The trays on this set were tuned by sanding the tray rails, smoothing the tray surfaces in contact with the tray, and applying talcum powder to the tray rail.

The straw board is susceptible to corner and edge damage, the layers will chip and separate, typical of particle board. The straw board seems to attract long legged spiders, disproportionately. On two occasions, the routing was stopped yielding a burn that continued to grow. The proximity of routing dust encouraged the burn to smolder just like a magnifying glass with sunlight being focused on the spot. This was surprising in the relatively high humidity environment of Seattle.

Consider making the back and sides 32" high rather than 29". This will raise the monitor more and leave more space inside the cabinet above the keyboard. The space is adequate for a keyboard but access is restricted, i.e. pulling the mouse in or retrieving items from behind the keyboard.. If heavy items are to be placed on the top, an overlay top could be added and supported by the sides and back. Currently, the top supports a 19" TV and the top deflects downward about 1/4". It would be desirable to double the thickness of the top but it would exceed the material available in a 4 x 8 sheet. Thus far there are no other indications of stress.

This project was started on 5.21.2001 and got to the point where the third coat of paint was needed on 6.7.2001. Although there were some interruptions and plans/documentation took some time, the project easily consumed 80 hours. Although the project is interesting in its application of the WorkBench, use of straw board, and the ROTOZIP®, as the work proceeded, the effort to complete this became obvious and the radial arm saw was used to cut the 1 x 2 skeleton members. In addition, I got sunburned twice, unheard of in Seattle. The materials and paint cost $50.00, not including the carpet casters.

The 3/8" by 4' square straw board is serving as chair mat a over carpet and as a mat under the Computer tables. In both cases, it allows the easy movement of the Computer Tables or Office Chair. The 4 x 4 squares were painted to match the carpet and it is larger than the mat it replaced. The 3/8" thickness seem to be the minimum thickness for a chair mat application.

by Joel N. Gessele

Appendix

Expanded Base:

Why would you want to add a large clumsy base to the ROTOZIP®? For primary uses of the ROTOZIP® Spiral Saw, the manufacturer's base is sufficient. When greater precision is desired an expanded base is necessary to assist in controlling the saw. The expanded base outlined here will assist in:
- ✓ Edge trimming
- ✓ Flush Trimming
- ✓ Rabbetting and Dadoing
- ✓ Table routing
- ✓ Ripping

C A U T I O N: Always consider the ROTOZIP®, Expanded Base, and Circle Cutter as separate pieces that can separate at the most inopportune time. Although the depth guide is twist/locked onto the ROTOZIP®, proceed with the expectation that the motor could separate from the depth guide. Use caution, the depth gauge set screw is easy to overpower even when checked and tightened carefully. The expanded base works best in situations where it is used to cut consistently and settings must be checked for accuracy with test cuts.

<u>Safety First...</u>
<u>Yada Yada Yada.</u>
<u>The Caution was written before I used the ROTOZIP®, thinking that it was a helpful suggestion, but not applicable to me. On the third cut, with the roundover bit, I elected to adjust the ROTOZIP® depth gauge, the cut proceeded with a 3" long gouge before I stopped cutting. An amazed, angry operator withdrew the ROTOZIP® to determine what was wrong. At that time, the depth gauge, and adjusting screw fell to the ground. If it was tightened, it was tightened askew and loosened on use.</u>
<u>Safety First...</u>
<u>At least two other instances were experienced, where one of the components changed position during use. Both were minor where the cutting depth changed. The same type of incident has occurred when using traditional routers. No damage or injury occurred in these two incidents. The Bracket, Board, and Stringer project has additional details on techniques for use with the Expanded Base.</u>

The expanded base attaches through the Circle Cutter. It allows precise adjustment of the portable fence by moving the base where it is attached to the Circle Cutter. The apex is the follower for routing detailed patterns. Three offsets are available when the edges are used as guides: a ~ 2.0" offset from the end. a ~2.5 " offset to the sides, and a ~5.6" offset from the apex sides. The offset to the apex is longer, it doesn't provide a flat surface for routing consistent widths, it provides a point for following intricate patterns.

by Joel N. Gessele

The material selected for the base is ¼ " thick. The base should not be used to move the ROTOZIP®, but only to guide the tool. The ¼ " material was chosen to make more of the length of the bits available. A relatively small ½ " hole for the bit exists in the expanded base because the ROTOZIP® should be considered as a light duty router and small diameter router bits used at the high standard 30,000 rpm speed. If a router bit is being used and it extends too far below the base, add a spacer as another layer on the base or shim strips.

The larger base allows the ROTOZIP® to remove material for insetting hinges, trim dowel ends, or level edge treatments. The fence can be used to position straight cut bits for rabbets, dadoes, or preparation of edges.

Fig. A-01: Top View of Expanded Base.

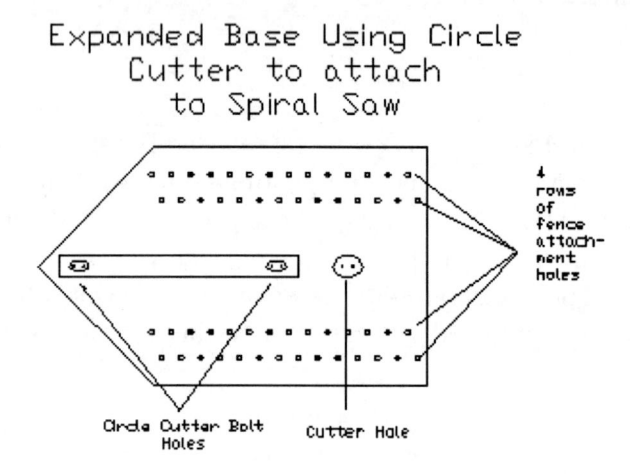

Plexiglass is recommended. Plexiglass will scratch with use and become opaque. The additional visibility of a clear material is initially useful when using the expanded base. The fence screws are offset allowing the fence to be installed even with the edges or protruding from the edge of the base. Installed in the protruding position, the fence is more visible and easier to position when cuts are started. Use the attached pattern it has been prepared to be accurate through the reproduction process over and above copying processes that may be less accurate. Check the pattern, make sure that the reproduction process has produced an accurate pattern. Check to make sure that the corners are square, that the fence holes are evenly spaced in two directions, across and in relationship to its neighbors and that the spline is ½ " wide..

A half inch wide strip is needed to support the base where it bolts to the circle cutter. At least two 5 15/16" 1/4" strips are needed, they are useful as duplicate fences, gauges, and may need replacement. Instructions for making the 1/4" Fence is included. Fences are easy to make. Various fences may be needed, don't hesitate to make one for your needs. When the first attempts to make Bureau Box Trays was attempted, the ¼ " fence was too thick. A thinner one was made to match the thickness of the plywood.

In use, the depth gauge is mounted to the Circle Cutter, and the Expanded Base to the Circle cutter. When using the assembly, it is easier to remove the depth gauge from the ROTOZIP® for assembly or disassembly. Taking the depth gauge off gives adequate room to adjust depth or clearances when a fence is installed in the Expanded Base.

If you haven't already searched for the lock washer on the depth gauge, now is the time to take preventative measures by putting a drop of glue on the lock washer. Even wood glue works, to keep the lock washer on the depth gauge adjustment screw. Losing the washer was initially a problem, as I worked with the ROTOZIP®, taking the depth gauge apart became less frequent and removal by twisting became the access method of choice.

Expanded Base: Cutting directions

1. Layout pattern on 1/4" Plexiglass (Available in Glass replacement section as Lucite).

2. Using a straight edge, cut out the base with the ROTOZIP®. There is a tendency to move the saw too slowly and melt rather than cut the plastic. Cut it, don't melt it.

by Joel N. Gessele

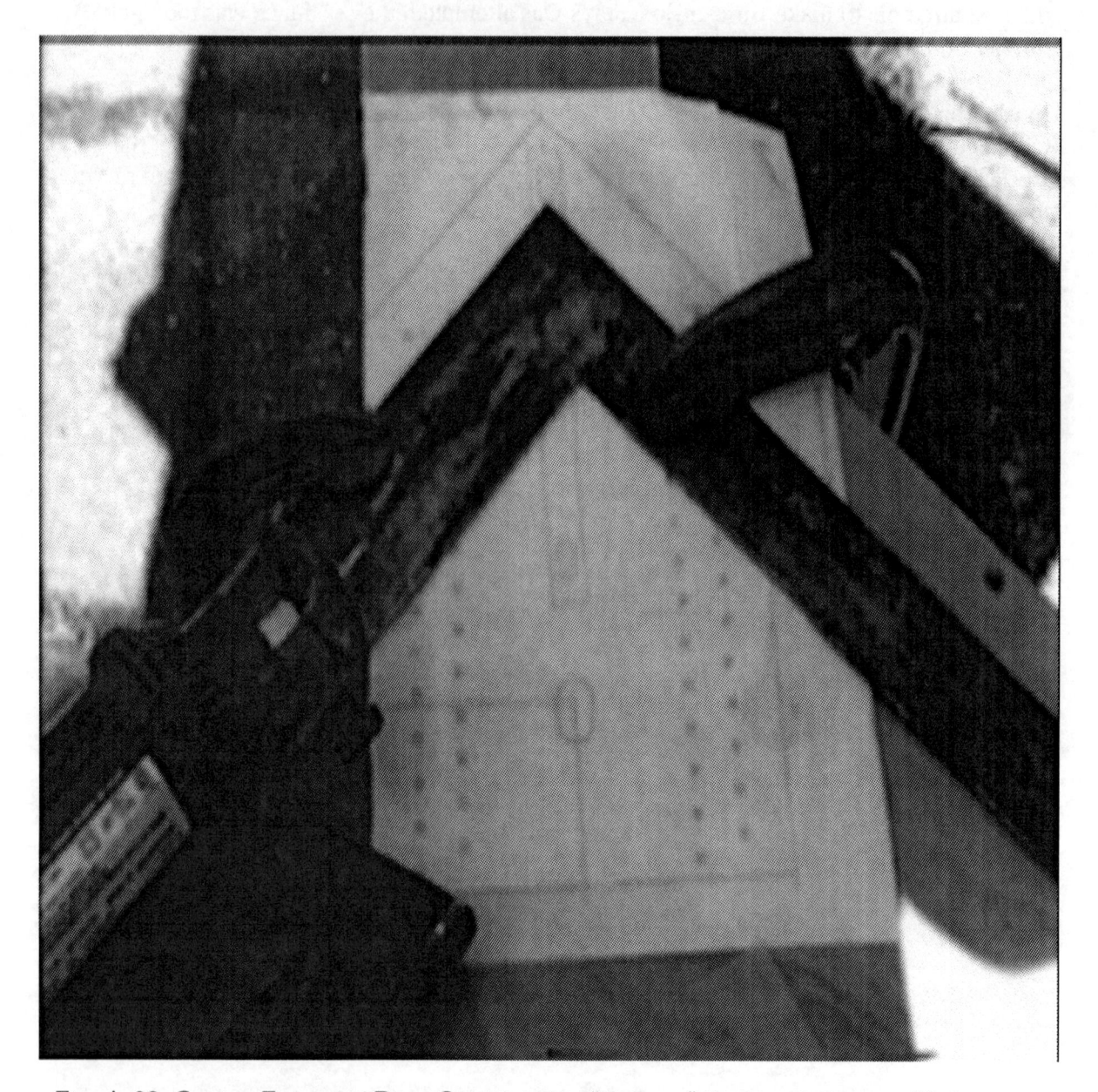

Fig, A-02: Cutting Expanded Base. Straight edge "protects" the item being cut. If the depth gauge isn't held down against the material and the straight edge it can run into the material. Prevent this by using a thicker fence rather than the convenient framing square. Side was cut with Framing Square protecting the base. Positioning the framing square for two cuts is too time consuming, position and cut one edge at a time. Positioning of clamps is critical.

3. Drill four rows of fence holes. A brad point drill bit was used to precisely position the bit on the dot inside the 1/8 " circle of the pattern.

4. Position a thick straight edge parallel to the center of the base. The thickness of the straight edge will allow you to plunge cut the center holes for attaching the Circle Cutter.

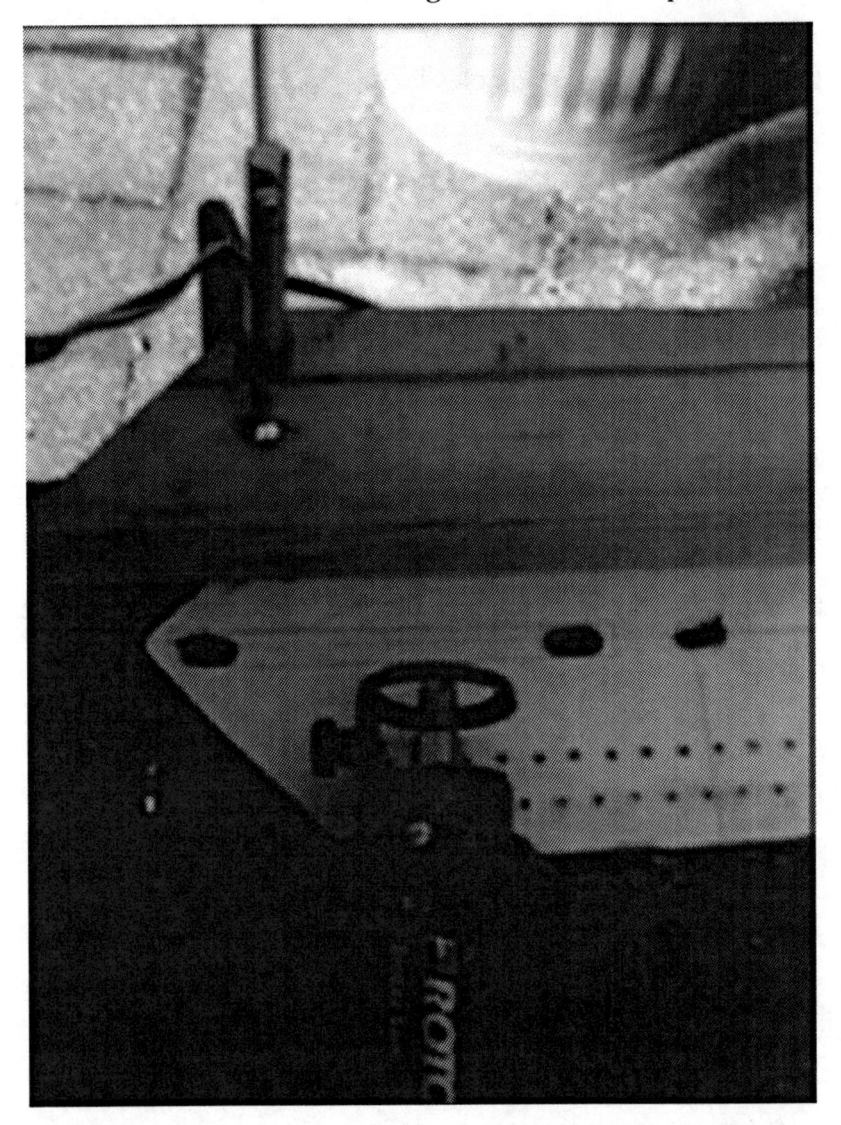

Fig. A-02 : Cutting center holes using 2 x 4 as straight edge and ¼ " Straight edge bit. Circle Cutter holes cut but not beveled. Bit hole will be enlarged to ½ " by freehand cutting.

Bevel the attachment holes using a counter sink bit matching the stove bolt heads' taper. Don't remove the Straight edge. The bevel must be smooth for easy adjustment and using the straight edge aids in making the sides of the bevel even.

5. Fences and a strip to fit inside the Circle Cutter handle(spline) can be cut from excess stock.

6. Glue strip to base. Plunge cut the holes through the Base plate.

by Joel N. Gessele

1/4" fence

7. Smooth and straighten the fence stock, drill stud holes for #4-40 x ¾ " machine screws using a 7/64 " bit.

8. Hacksaw the heads off two #4-40 x ¾ " machine screws and glue (epoxy preferred) them into the fence.

9. Smooth edges, square surfaces, and check the fence holes to make sure that the fence(s) fit all holes.

10. The Expanded Base is attached to the circle cutter with ¼ -20 x ¾ Stove Bolts. Wing nuts are used to allow hand tightening when fence clearances are adjusted. The circle cutter is designed to rotate easily, now it needs to hold a position. Put a paper shim in the form of a washer between the circle cutter and the bottom of the depth gauge. This will tighten up the assembly and keep it from rotating, changing the settings. When using the Expanded Base in the WorkBench, the shims should be present and tightened enough to prevent the ROTOZIP® from rotating when switched on.

Notes on WorkBench:
- The washer /nut combinations were replaced with T-nuts on subsequent versions. The holes for the material clamp were moved to go through 1 x 2 edge into T-nuts on the 1 x 2..
- The 1 x 2 edge was attached pinwheel style and the wild ends cut off with the ROTOZIP® and a guidepoint bit. Start with a 1 x 2 inset from the corner ¾ inch. Glue and screw the 1 x 2 along the edge. Complete the perimeter by butting the end of the next 1 x 2 against the side of the first. Cut the wild ends off and glue and install a drywall screw through the butt joints at the corners.
- The small ¼ x ¼ x 6 portable fence has been replaced by larger fences attached to the expanded base.
- The WorkBench and the Expanded base will give good results where a consistent cut is needed. It is necessary to evaluate a test cut before committing to project cuts.

Expanded Base: Ripping

On small parts, moving the part past the bit is a practical solution for cutting parts to size. A larger piece can be cut with a longer straight edge clamped to the stock. Some repetitive cuts can be made with the portable fence bolted to the Expanded base.

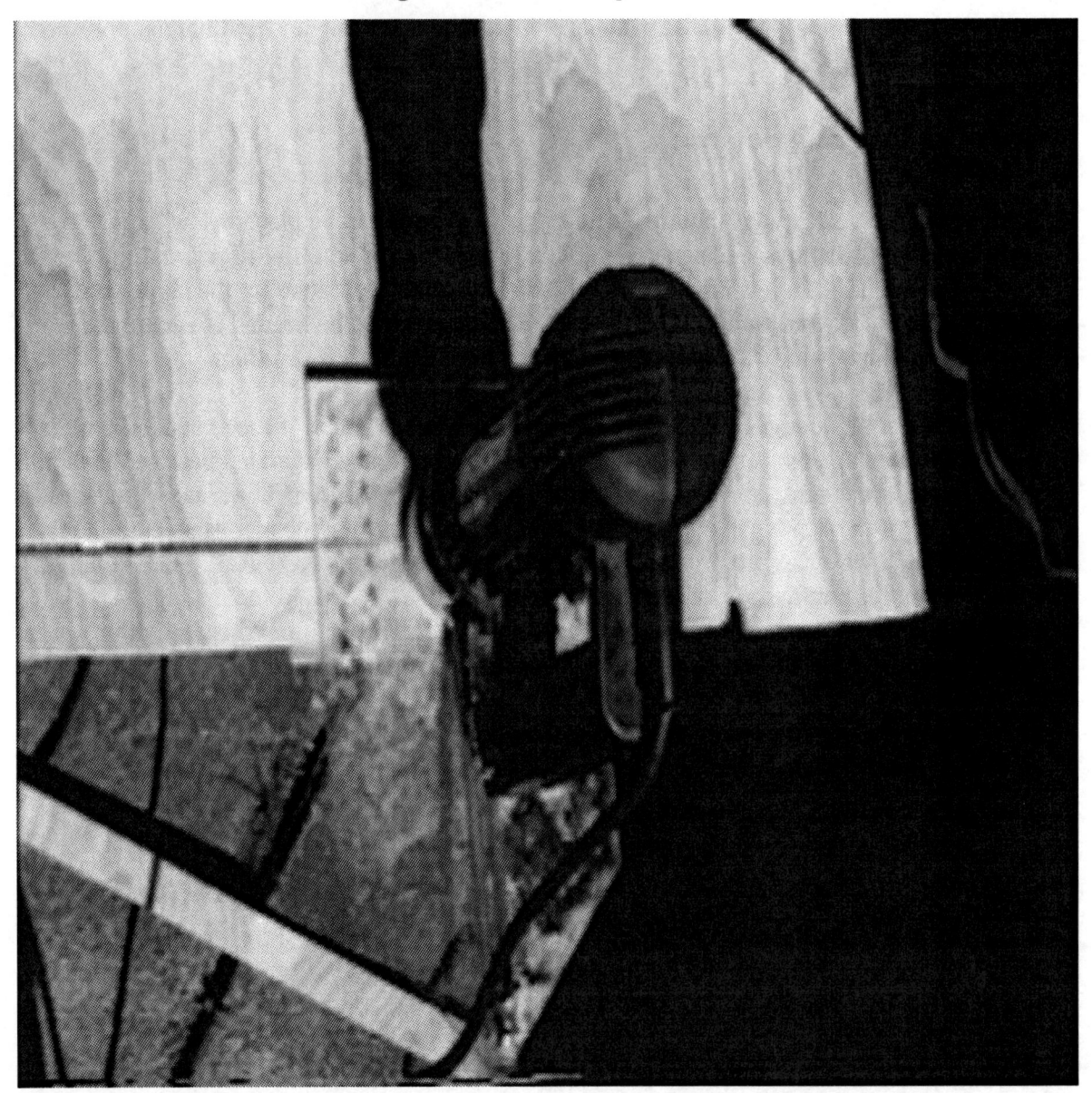

Fig. A-03: Ripping with portable fence. Partially completed cross grain rip on 1/4" plywood. Portable fence is attached to Expanded Base and 1/4" fence is against the plywood to create 1 1/2" strips.

Expanded Base: Stopped Dadoes

Stopped dadoes or grooves are preferred where dadoes meet joint corners. The Stopped dado leaves material in the corner for the rabbet joint. If the dado was run to the edge of the material, a hole would appear in the completed joint or at the edge of a panel.

Make stopped dadoes by lowering the stock onto the straight cut bit. A mark on the fence can provide a reference for the location of the bit. Marks including the offset are useful if

by Joel N. Gessele

several stopped dadoes need to be made and a consistent starting and ending positions are needed.

Speed or Framing Square:

Selection of a cutoff square should consider where clamps can be placed. The larger commercially available speed squares provide more area and stability for clamping. The framing square used in several projects provided adequate clearance for the clamp and didn't get in the way of the ROTOZIP®. Multiple clamps may be needed to secure the parts. Use clamps to hold the parts and to secure the parts for safe cutting.

The use of a straight edge to make straight or square cuts is useful if the expanded base is used or the depth gauge edge is used carefully. When using the expanded base or the depth gauge, precautions must be taken to keep the orientation consistent. The small variations of the distance of the depth gauge ring or the circle cutter edge may be inconsequential most of the time. However, when precise straight cuts are needed, the ROTOZIP® must not be rotated when the cut is made. Marks on the depth gauge ring can aid in keeping the orientation consistent. Keeping the position of the ROTOZIP® motor constant with respect to the expanded base will serve the same purpose and give precise cuts.

When using the framing square as a guide, occasionally the guide may rise above the edge and notch the material. A thick speed square, framing square, or fence helps avoid this and if very thick, permits plunge cutting.

Setup Spacer

A strip of plexiglass the same width as the distance from the edge of the depth gauge to the bit is very useful for positioning the straight edge. One of the Spacer edges is placed on the marks of the cut to be made. The straight edge is then clamped against the other side.

A spacer can be made cutting a strip of plexiglass placed next to a 1 x 2. Another Spacer should be cut that is 1/8 " wider for use when an allowance for the width of the bit is needed. Make a test alignment and test cut to familiarize yourself with the resultant tolerances. An additional check can be made before a cut is made by placing the ROTOZIP® in position and checking the notches inside the edge of the depth gauge that mimic the 1/8 " bit, versus the line on the material. If accurate measurements are made, the width of the setup spacer for 1/8" bits is 15/16", half of the 2" diameter depth gauge minus one half the diameter of the ROTOZIP® bit.

WorkBench

A plywood square was used as a WorkBench. A work surface that was small and portable was needed. The uses and features of the WorkBench evolved as ROTOZIP® projects were tried. The specifications for a 2' x 2' WorkBench that fits on top of a galvanized garbage can are presented here.

Taming the ROTOZIP® Spiral Saw

Fig. A-04: WorkBench top view with ROTOZIP, expanded base, and material clamp.

The uses of features in the WorkBench are mentioned in the ROTOZIP® projects. Two methods of holding the WorkBench were used, a weight on the surface or two water filled gallon jugs suspended underneath the top on a cord. The 2' square plywood is appropriate for a conventional garbage can. Different sizes may be tried to get a higher or larger work surface, make sure that your selection will be safe and that at least 2" clearance around the top exists for the clamp bolts.

by Joel N. Gessele

Fig. A-05: WorkBench bottom view, showing Expanded base support strips attached to bottom. The counter sunk screw holes were not used because glue and weighting eliminated the need to screw the support strips to the top. Circle cutter attaching the ROTOZIP® to Expanded base, bottom view.

A cutout for the Expanded base and support strips was added to hold the base level with the bench surface. The Bench and the Expanded Base are needed to make dados and rabbet joints. The support strips and balance tabs can be seen in Fig, A-1-4.

WorkBench: Materials
   24" x 24" x ¼ " Plywood Square
    1" x 2 " x 8'   straight, fir or pine lumber for frame
    1" x 2 " x 6'   straight, fir or pine lumber for support strips

Taming the ROTOZIP® Spiral Saw

1" x 2" x16" straight, fir or pine lumber for clamp bar
16 - 1" drywall screws
Wood Glue.

WorkBench: Tools
¼ " drill bit, 1/8 " drill bit, drill,
Counter sink bit or equivalent large diameter bit.

WorkBench: Accessories
Framing square
¼ -20 threaded rod at least 6 "
2 ¼ - 20 wing nuts, 6 ¼ - 20 nuts, 6 - ¼ washers.
Epoxy for nut/washer application to clamping bolt holes.
Cord, at least 4 feet.
Gallon Jugs
Permanent marker

WorkBench: Blueprint

Fig. A-06:

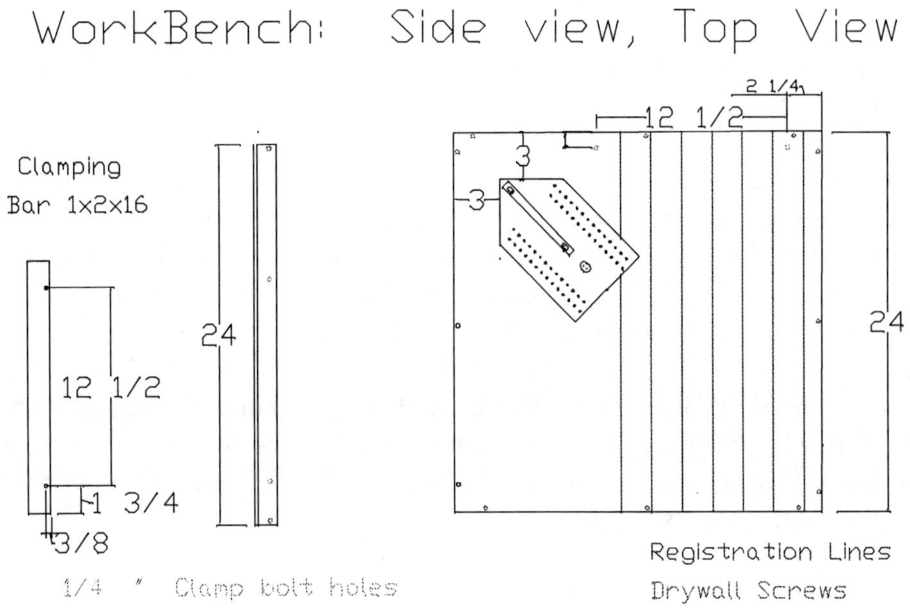

WorkBench: Side view, Top View

WorkBench: Frame
The plywood square was edged with 1x2's (actual 3/4" x 1 1/2"). The edging makes the bench stiffer and provides a substantial clamping surface. The 1 x 2's were attached with

by Joel N. Gessele

drywall screws, three to a side, through predrilled, countersunk holes and glue. A screw was added at each corner, joining the edge 1x2 to the end 1x2. Instead of detailed instructions, just assemble the frame components without bending the top by forcing tight joints or rolling the top with short frame members. An alternative to two 24 " members and two 22 ½ " members would be four 23 ¼ " members installed sequentially around the perimeter of the plywood square.

WorkBench: Expanded Base
Inverting the ROTOZIP® and placing it in the work bench allows a large number of table routing operations to be performed. The unattached inverted base is placed on a diagonal line of the bench top. The expanded base is centered over the diagonal line. The sides of the Expanded Base cutter apex are 3 inches from sides of the bench top. An outline of the base is drawn on the bench top and cut out by clamping a framing square to guide the ROTOZIP®. A snug fit is desired and a little hand work to obtain the desired fit is suggested. The expanded base is custom made. It is necessary to custom fit the cutout. Hopefully, the base and the WorkBench will have equal lifetimes.

The expanded base is supported by support strips glued to the underside of the work bench. The thickness of the support strips is determined by the ROTOZIP® power cord diameter. The support strips must be thicker than the power cord so that the bench doesn't pinch the cord when the ROTOZIP® is inverted and placed in the WorkBench by the garbage can. In addition to the support strips, two balance strips are needed to prevent the bench from rocking. The balance strips are the two short strips glued to the bottom, at right angles to the support strips (see Fig. A-05).

The diagonal orientation reserves a major portion of the bench top for work. The point of the expanded base is accessible from the edge and allows the base and ROTOZIP® to be tipped onto the surface for adjustment or removal. A power strip is used as an auxiliary power switch when the ROTOZIP® is inverted in the WorkBench. Although the power strip's switch was an easy way to turn the power off and on when the ROTOZIP® was in the table , it caused a problem when I took it out of the WorkBench. Several times, I took the ROTOZIP® out of the WorkBench, set it up for another operation, and plugged it back in, WITH THE ROTOZIP® SWITCH ON. Avoid this situation, the surprise is not enjoyable and it is dangerous. Please remember to turn the switch off when you take it out of the table by whatever method that works for you..

WorkBench: Weighting
Part of the purpose of building a WorkBench is to provide a portable work surface. The light materials used in the bench make it easy to pickup and store. It does not instill confidence when it moves around when you use it. Drill holes at opposite sides of the frame for a cord to suspend water filled gallon jugs. Drill the holes close to the underside of the WorkBench top. Do not put a cord hole on the same frame member as the clamp holes. Tie a knot in the cord and thread the end under the bench. Run the cord through the handles of filled gallon jugs. Complete the weighting by threading the cord out the hole in the opposite frame member. Add weight by shortening the cord, lifting the gallon jugs, and

knotting the cord to suspend the jugs. If the garbage can is used exclusively for ROTOZIP® projects, it can store the gallon jugs, the sawdust, the wood scraps, the plans, patterns, tools and broken bits, just don't let the garbage pickup get hold of it!

WorkBench: Clamp

Many operations need stock to be clamped for cutting or routing. In addition, it is desirable to have a straight edge to guide the cut. A simple clamp was added to the work bench to hold stock and make right angle cuts. The basic component of the clamp is a 1x2x16 and two ¼ - 20 x 3 threaded rod. Wing Nuts and glue were used rather than knobs to permit easy assembly of the clamp parts. Glue the wing nuts to the threaded rod or use a wing nut and a burr makes a temporary attachment to the threaded rod. A nut and washer were glued to the under or back sides of both pairs of clamping holes. Crazy glue is adequate for all three applications. When one of the four nut/washers assemblies broke loose, it was reattached with epoxy and the others reinforced. A better approach is to use T-nuts - See Notes at the end of the WorkBench above.

Two orientations for clamping were devised, vertical and horizontal. The 1x2x16 has holes drilled 3/8" from the edge rather than in its center. This allows the clamping bar to be placed in several orientations providing a flush edge or an offset edge when used as a vertical clamp. The holes were marked and drilled in the bar. The bar was then used as a template to drill the holes in the WorkBench surface and frame by using C-clamps to hold it in position and drilling through the holes.

The table is marked with parallel lines at right angles to the 1x2x16 when used as a horizontal clamping bar. This permits the horizontal orientation to be used as right angle guide for crosscutting. The clamping bar must extend over the edge for crosscutting operations and the edge of the bar marked to assure that the right angle lines match the surface used for crosscutting. When you mark the lines, be sure that the primary edge and orientation are used to mark the parallel lines. Do not assume that the clamping bar's edges are parallel or that edge of the table is parallel the clamping bar. Check the setup with the framing square before marking.

WorkBench: Fence

Two types of fences were used, a portable one attached to the expanded base or one clamped to the WorkBench. Both have advantages. The fence bolted to the expanded base is portable and the settings are retained even if the depth gauge is removed. A fence clamped across the WorkBench is easy to adjust and simple.

A simple portable Fence is useful for many operations. The simplest fence is a ¾ " board with a straight edge. Holes are drilled to match the rows of fence holes. Putting the holes for all four rows of fence holes will allow an incremental adjustment for all conditions. The holes should be parallel the fence in line with the rows of fence holes in the Expanded

by Joel N. Gessele

Base. All four holes in the fence must be the same distance from the working edge of the fence, otherwise the amount of adjustment is reduced. The portable ¼ " fence with bolts epoxied into the fence involves more preparation but it is convenient and compact.

A fence clamped across the WorkBench is easier to adjust than the portable fence. However it is more difficult to adjust depth and retain a fence position with the clamped fence.

WorkBench: Guidepoint Flush Trimming

Flush trimming on projects is easier and less risky when the ROTOZIP® is mounted in the WorkBench. The Bureau Box, Bureau Box Tray, and the Magazine Box all have end joints that may benefit from flush trimming. The Bureau Box Tray is a beneficiary of the trimming process on ends, and edges.. When the tongue and groove are removed by trimming, the excess glue is removed and a finished edge created. A smoother edge and consistent angle is easier to get when the Expanded Base and the WorkBench are used.

The cutting steps have been arranged to allow for minute adjustments for actual cuts. One of the dimensions that is most affected by actual conditions are the rabbet joints on top and bottom panels. If the dado is too large, the cross grain dado to end rabbet has a large unsightly gap. If the top/bottom rabbet has too much cut out, a gap between the panel and the case results and the case may not be square when assembled. Complete the case dadoes and grooves before cutting the top/bottom panels. The actual dimensions for the rabbets are transferred from the completed case parts. If the top/bottom panel was cut too large, the excess can easily be sanded off the panel because the tenon that remains is less than 1/8" thick.

Fig. A-06: Flush Trim setup tips:

Flush Trim Adjustment

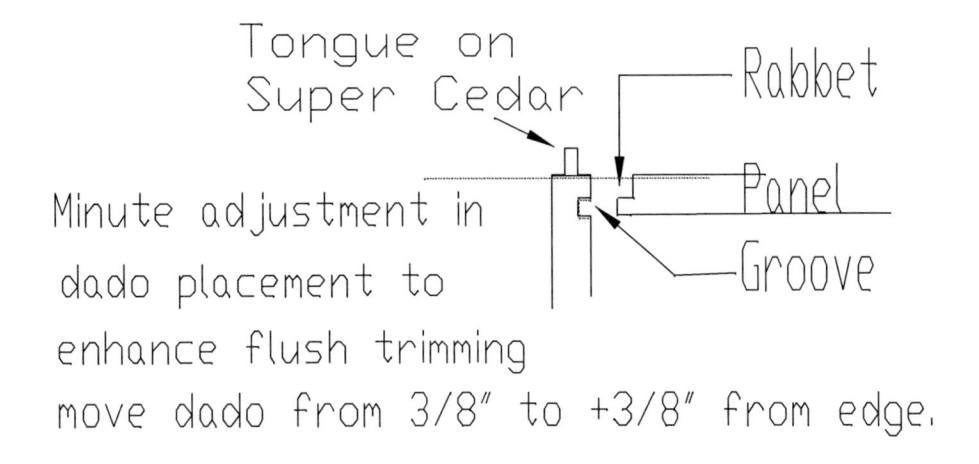

Tongue on Super Cedar — Rabbet — Panel — Groove

Minute adjustment in dado placement to enhance flush trimming move dado from 3/8" to +3/8" from edge.

The most frequent application of flush trimming is the removal of the tongue and groove on parts made from Super Cedar Closet Lining. The Bureau Box Tray has excess material between the bottoms and trimming is not a concern for the depth of the box. The same is not true for the length of the Bureau Box Tray. Make an allowance for the trimming operation when you cut the part to length and cut cross grain dado. The final dimension is dependent on the width of the dado, the thickness of the rabbet, and the thickness of the material used for the end panel.

When the joint is measured and adjustments made for cutting the dado, consider the effects of trimming and make allowances to get the final tolerances after trimming. Moving the dado away from the edge will eliminate ghosting of the tongue or groove when trimmed. Moving the position of the dado can alter the dimensions of the final project and complicate final fitting. The advantage of trimming is a precise edge for less time and less effort. If you plan to trim a joint and move the dado further away from the edge, cut the part longer to compensate for the trimming step. The Bureau Box Tray and the Bureau Box have Tongue and Groove trimming operations, but the trimming affects less critical dimensions. Critical dimensions that are trimmed at the edge trimming of the Bureau Box Trays, too short and drops off the rails, too long and it won't fit in the Bureau Box. Don't overreact, there is a full 3/8 " variance that will still make usable trays.

by Joel N. Gessele

This page intentionally left blank.

0
#4-40 x ¾, 107
¼ -20 x ¾ Stove Bolts, 107

1
1/8 " dowels, 4

2
2 foot panel, 50
2 foot stock, 50

4
4 foot stock, 50

A
Amber shellac, 57

B
balance strips, 113
box knife, 56
Bracket, Board and Stringer Shelf, 72
brad point drill bit, 55, 105

C
case parts
    Computer Table, 86
case splitting, 53
catch, 61
CD rack, 72
chair mat, 86, 100
Chamfer bit,, 75
channel
    clasp, 55
Circle Cutter
    Expanded Base, 102
Computer Table, 85
cord, 110, 113
Cross cutting, 24

D
depth gauge screw, 81
dual display systems., 85

E
Edge trimming, 35, 51

F
Fence, 114
    Particle board, 77
    portable fence, 102
Flush Trim, 115
flush trimming, 116
framing square, 109
    guide, 109

G
gallon jug, 110, 113
gallon jugs, 50
glue spills, 50
guidepoint bit, 3

H
hacksaw blade-handle, 93

I
insetting hinges, 103

J
jewelry file
    file, 70

K
keyboard tray, 86

L
level edge treatments, 103
lid retainer brackets, 54

O
outlet covers, 69

P
particle board, 86
    Strawboard, 86
pattern underneath, 4
plexiglass
    spacer, 109
plunge cut, 67, 105
plunge cutting, 109
plywood square, 109
portable fence, 114
portable work surface, 113
power strip, 113

R
Rechargeable screwdriver, 61
roundover bit, 102
rubber bands, 50, 52

S
Safety, 102
sash chain, 52
sealer, 99
shellac
    sealer, 99
Spacer, 109
speed square, 109
Stacking shelves
    stackers, 85
Stopped dadoes, 108
stopped grooves, 51
straight cut router bit, 51
Strawboard, 86
strawboard,, 85
support strips, 113

T

tray rail, 43
tray rails, 50, 52
triangular file
    file, 70
trim dowel ends, 103
trimming, 58

W

wax paper, 50
weight, 110
width limit for ripping panels, 86
wood clasp, 56
wooden clasp, 55
WorkBench
    Cross Cutting, 24

About the Author

My experience has been gained by building routing tables, templates, furniture, a boat, remodeling homes, and automobile reconditioning. The experience was applied to solve application, construction, and materials problems using the ROTOZIP ® for atypical projects. The experience is used to exploit the core technology of the Spiral Saw to projects that expand its uses. The projects are selected on how well the Spiral Saw and materials can be used to build the projects while saving on total investment in tools, materials, work space, clean up time, and preparation time.

The detailed instructions and illustrations are a result of experience in detailing procedures for repeatable processes, in this case, for projects that reflect craftsmanship and beauty. The projects are developed in IntelliCAD® by CADopia. The use of a CAD package improves the quality of the plans by dimensioning the drawing, encouraging the consideration of options, and allowing the printing of patterns and templates. The development of the plan, writing of the procedure, constructing the project, finishing the project, using the project, and critiquing the project are parts of a process that is necessary for creating build able projects. Projects are not handed off to someone where the complications of a design are not immediately and directly experienced in building the project. The experience of completing the project, based on the directions, is immediately improved in design and directions for subsequent builders.

Many of the projects are presented as demonstrations for "What if I used" proposals for solving problems or the use of commercial materials. The use of commercially available aromatic cedar is used to build medium sized boxes that have cases that are in proportion to their purpose and size. The shelf conserves wood and provides functionality with a moveable center section. The outlet covers are included as a common item that has customization possibilities when they can be made quickly and easily. I have tried to select projects that present solutions and encourage readers to apply the solutions to new problems by including an analysis of the completed project and procedure in the Results sections.

by Joel N. Gessele

Directory of Plans and Patterns for:
Taming the ROTOZIP Spiral Saw

The Plans and Patterns have been appended to allow printing of sets of project plans on 8 1/2" x 11" paper. Please confirm that the **patterns** are true to scale by checking at least one dimension.

Project:	Title:	Page: +
Wood Bull Bank	Face Pattern	125
Wood Bull Bank	Head Pattern	126
Wood Bull Bank	Horn Section Pattern	127
Wood Bull Bank	Back Section Pattern	128
Wood Bull Bank	Bridge and Middle Nose Pattern	129
Wood Bull Bank	Nose Pattern	130
Wood Bull Bank	Horn Patterns	131
Magazine Box	Plan for sides and ends	132
Magazine Box	Plan for top/bottom	133
Bureau Box Tray	Plan for Side	134
Bureau Box Tray	Plan for End	135
Bureau Box Tray	Plan for Top/Bottom	136
Bureau Box	Plan for Side	137
Bureau Box	Plan for End and Top/Bottom	138
Bureau Box	Pattern for Sash Chain Lid Retainer	139
Bureau Box	Pattern for Clasp	140
Bracket, Board, and Stringer Shelf	Shelf Profile	141
Bracket, Board, and Stringer Shelf	Shelf Bracket, and Stringer Plans	142
Bracket, Board, and Stringer Shelf	Template for Stringer	143
Computer Table	Cutting Diagram for Computer Table	144
Computer Table	Hand Hold Template	145
Computer Table	Plan for Top	146
Computer Table	Plan for Back	147
Computer Table	Plan for Side	148
Computer Table	Plan for Bottom	149
Computer Table	Plan for Keyboard Tray	150
Computer Table	Plan for Stacker	151
Expanded Base	Expanded Base Pattern	152
WorkBench	Plan for WorkBench	153

Face

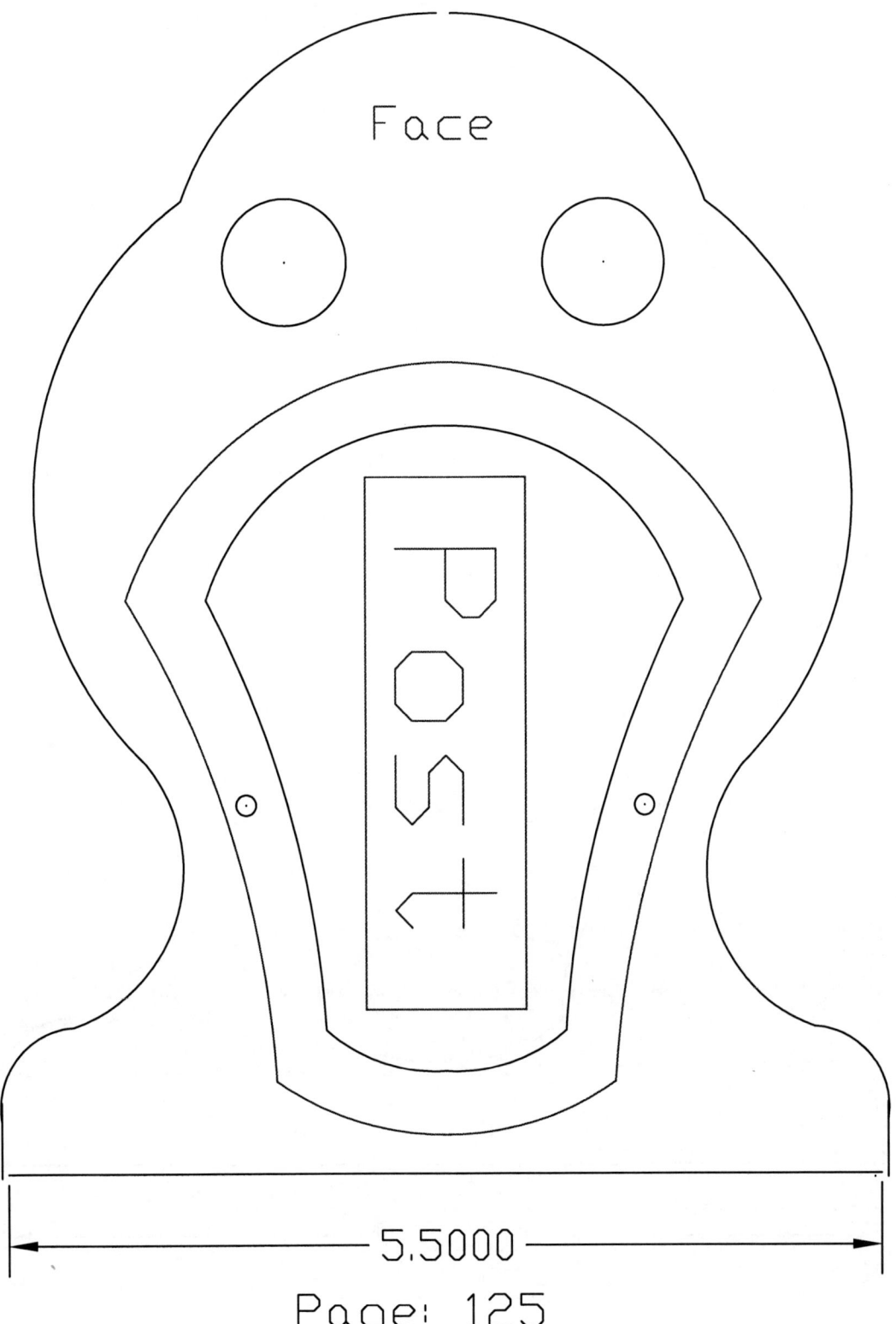

Post

5.5000

Page: 125

Head

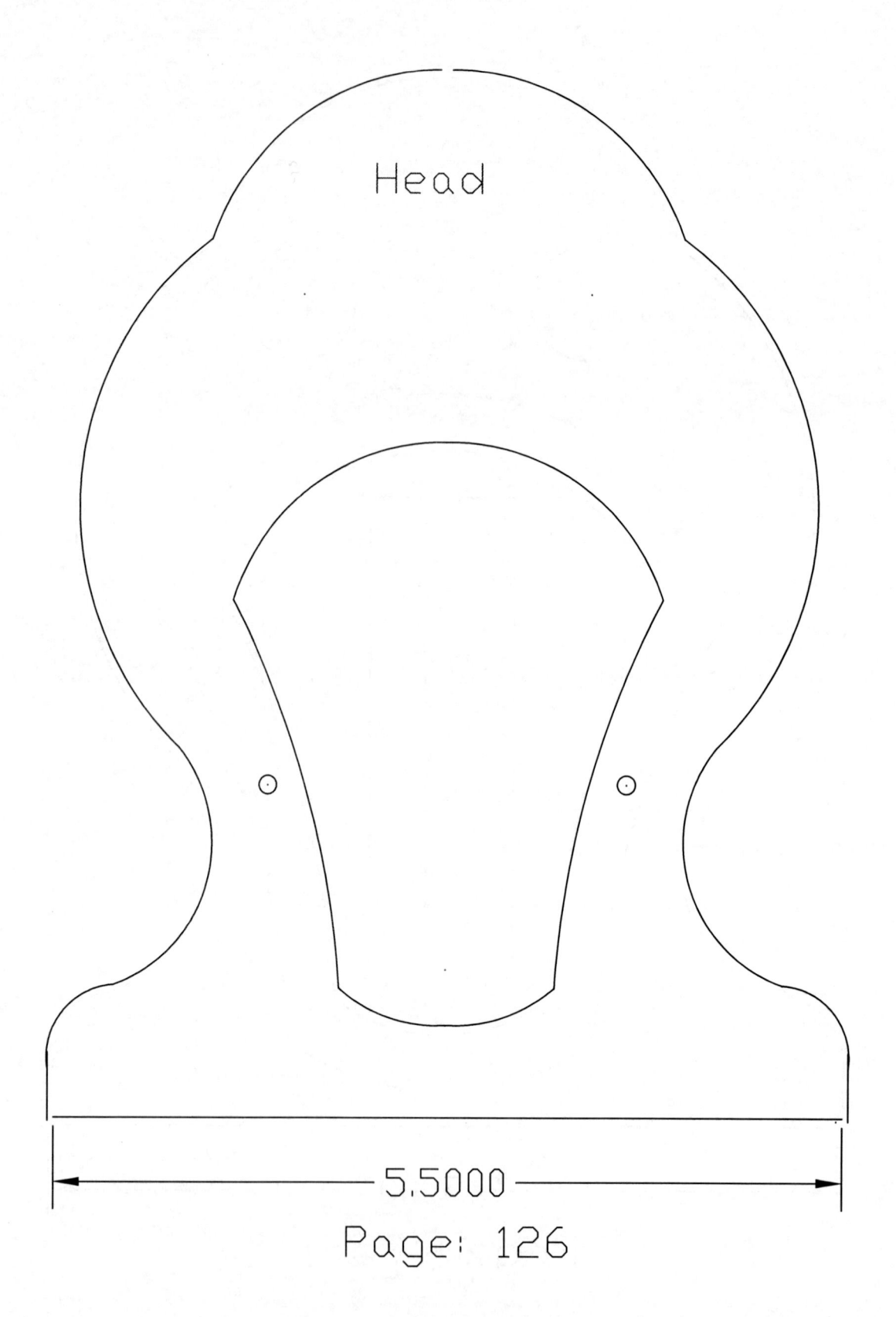

5.5000

Page: 126

Horn Section

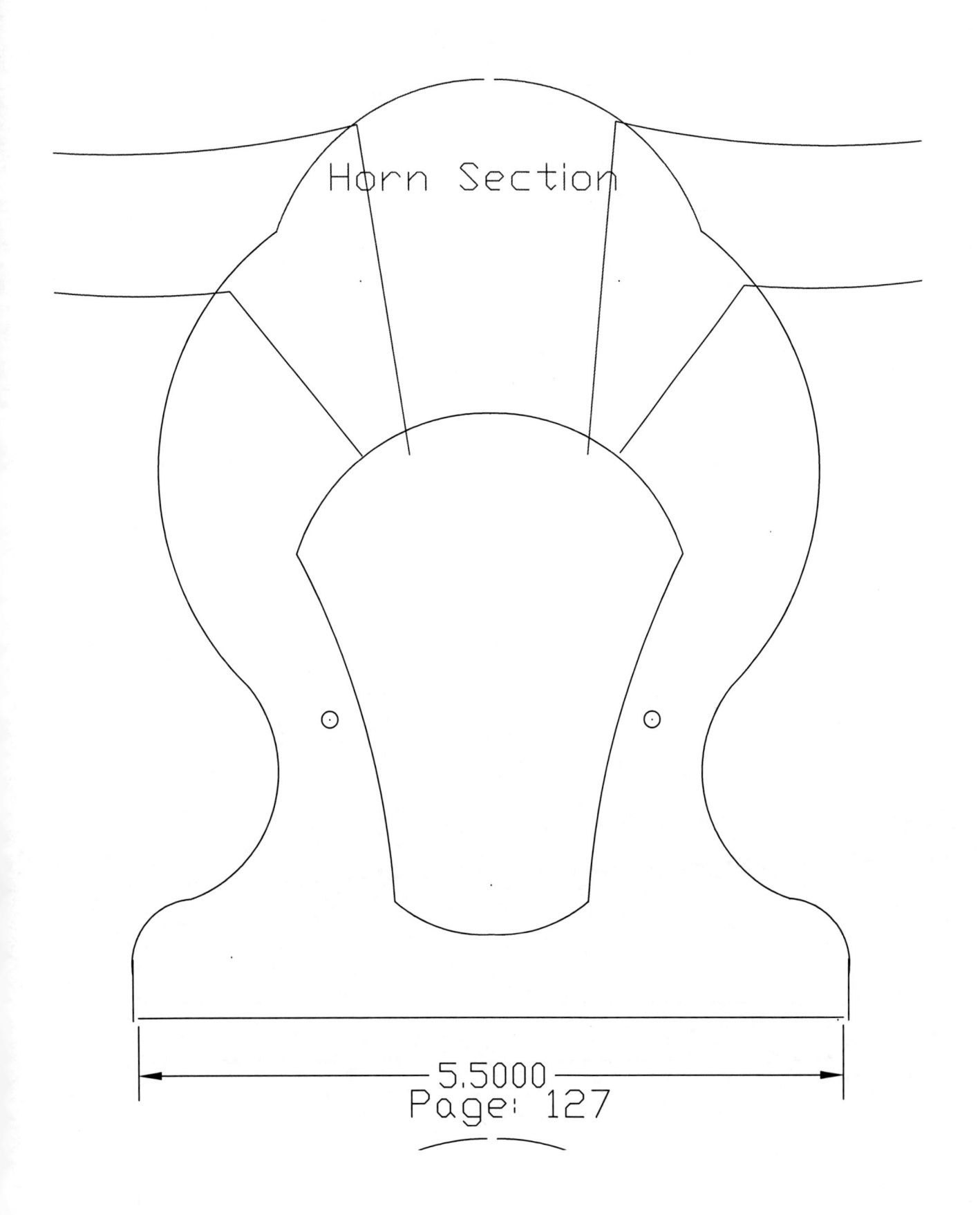

5.5000
Page: 127

Back

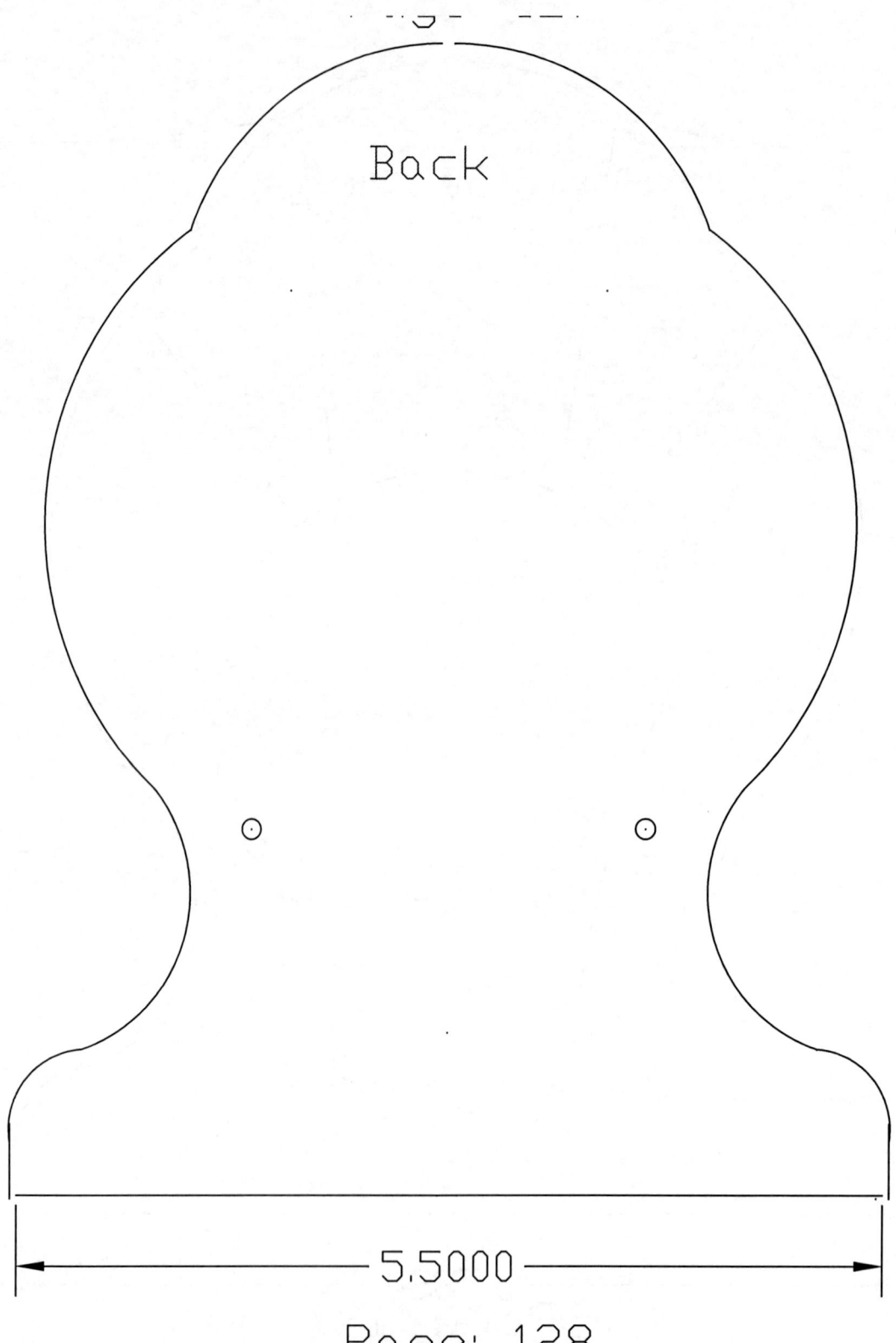

5.5000

Page: 128

Bridge

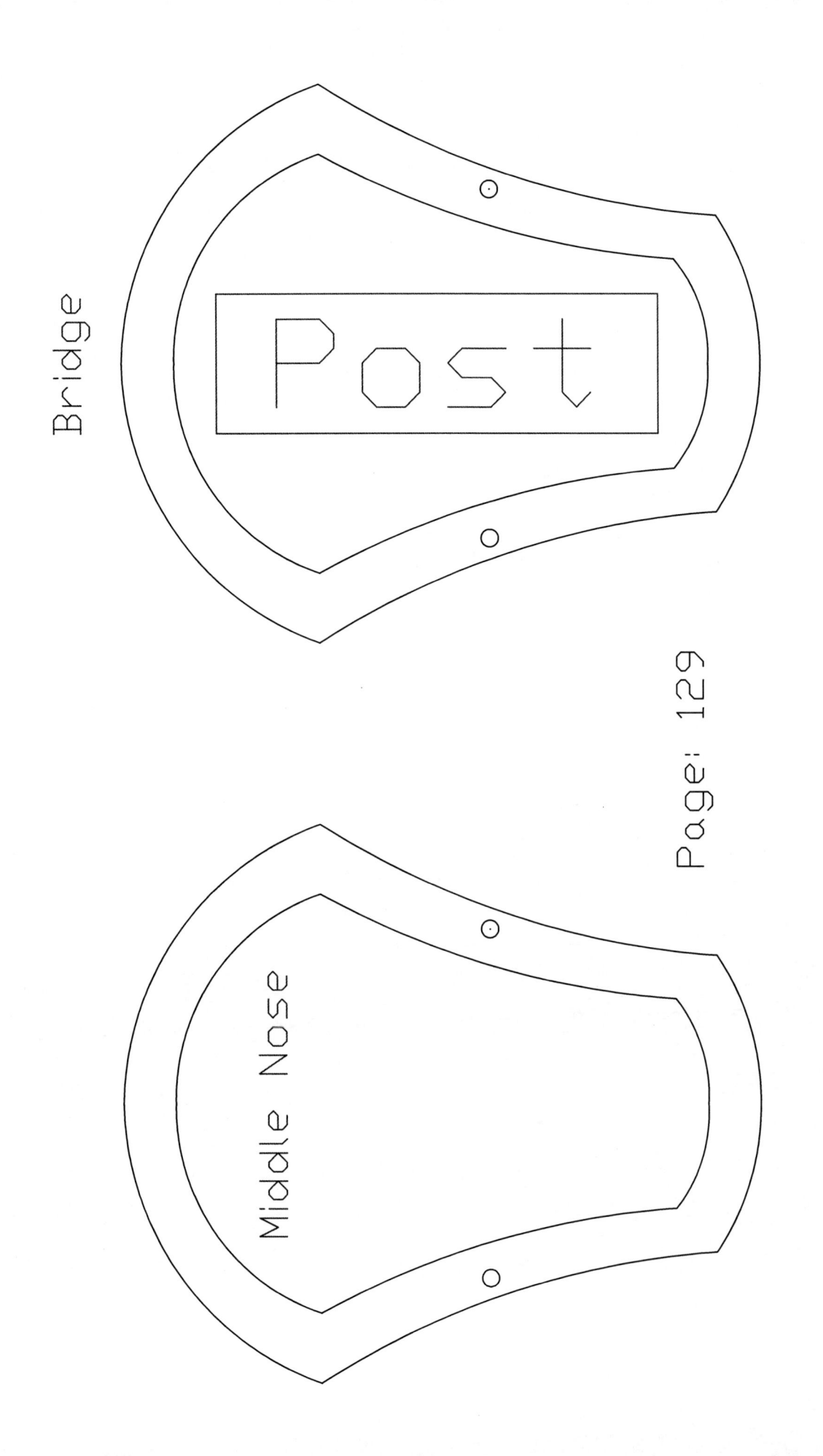

Post

Middle Nose

Page: 129

Nose

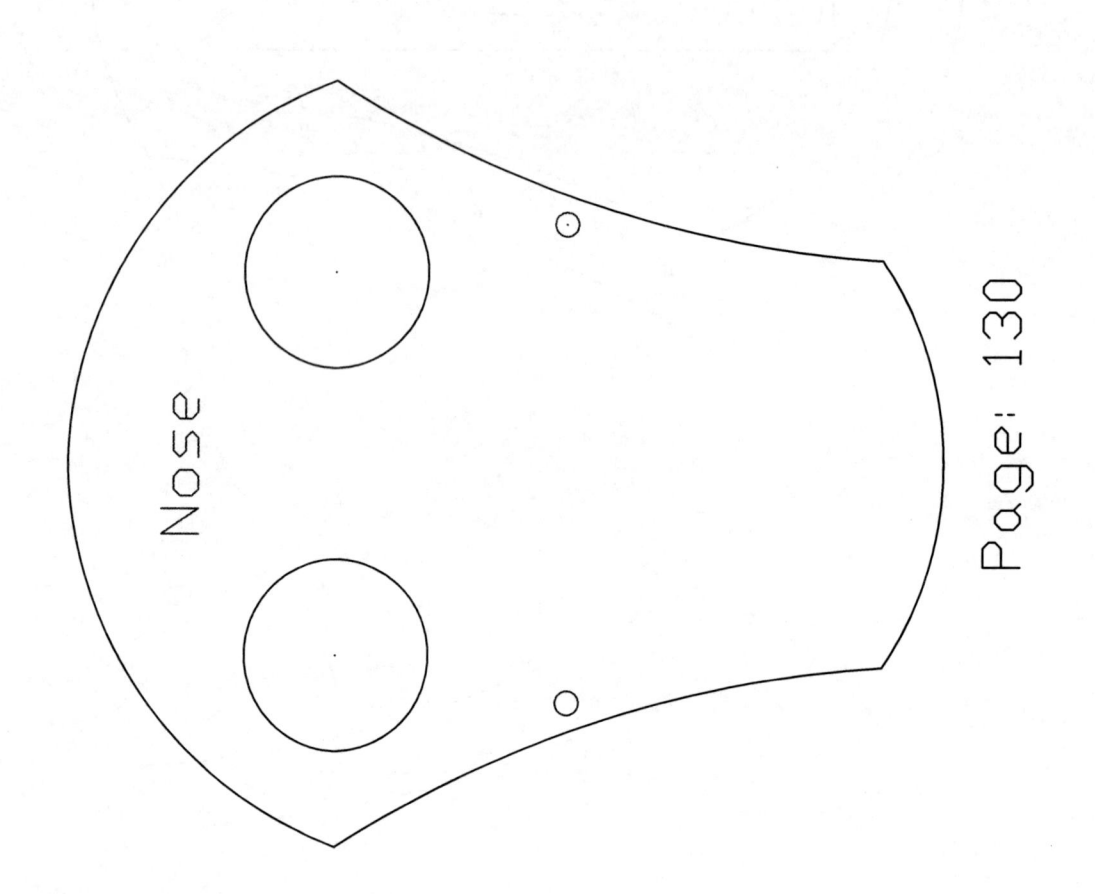

Page: 130

Long Horns

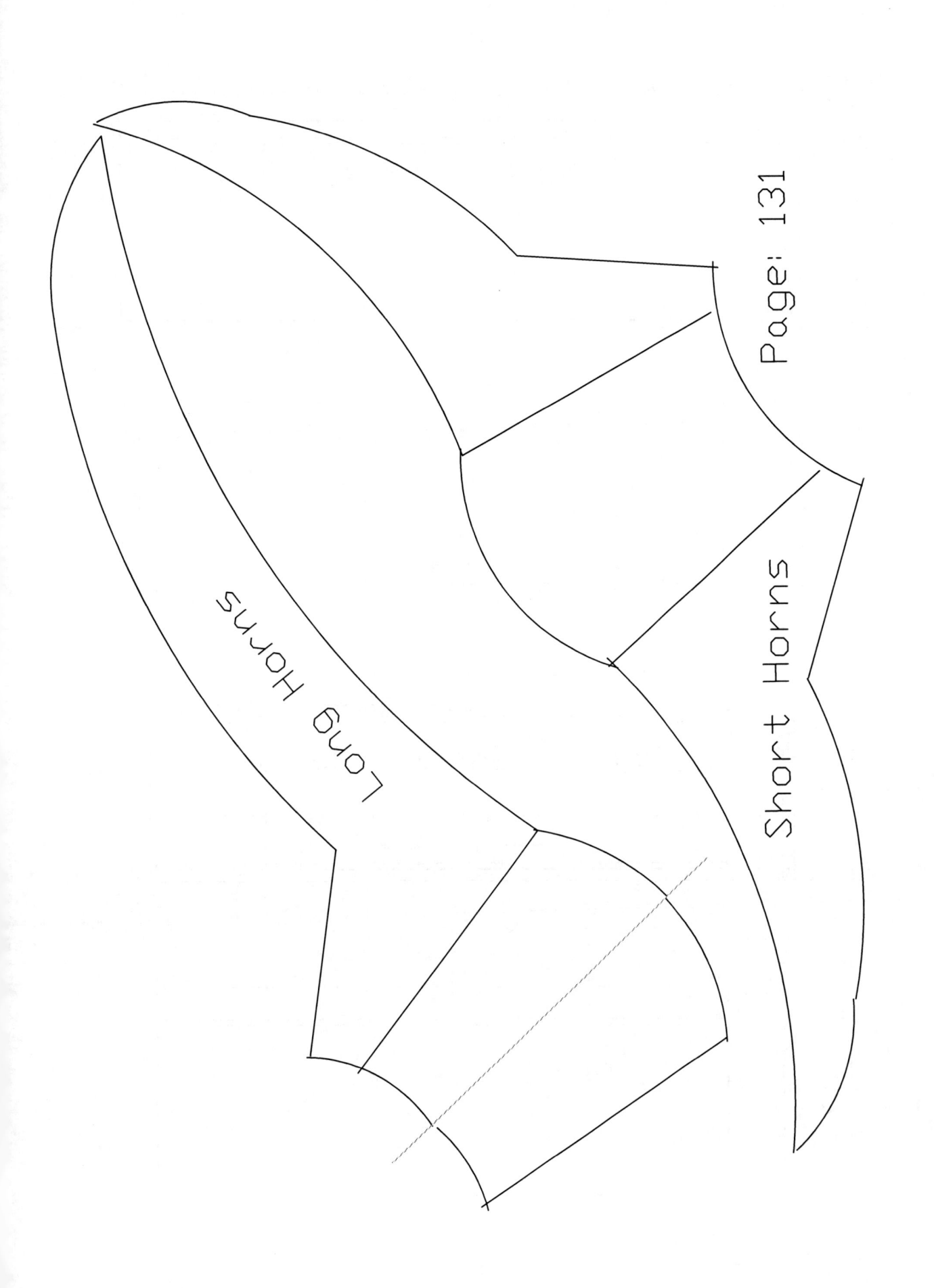

Short Horns

Page: 131

Magazine Box : End, Sides, Back, and Front

Side, Outside View
- 13.0 (13")
- 3.75 (3 3/4")
- 1/4"

Side, Inside View
- 13.0 (13")
- 3.75 (3 3/4")
- 3" Internal Clearance
- Cross Grain Dado
- Stopped Groove

Back - Inside View
- 12 3/4
- 3.75 (3 3/4")
- Cross Grain Rabbet - Face
- Through Groove

Front
- 12 1/2
- 3.75 (3 3/4")

Magazine Box: Top/Bottom outside view

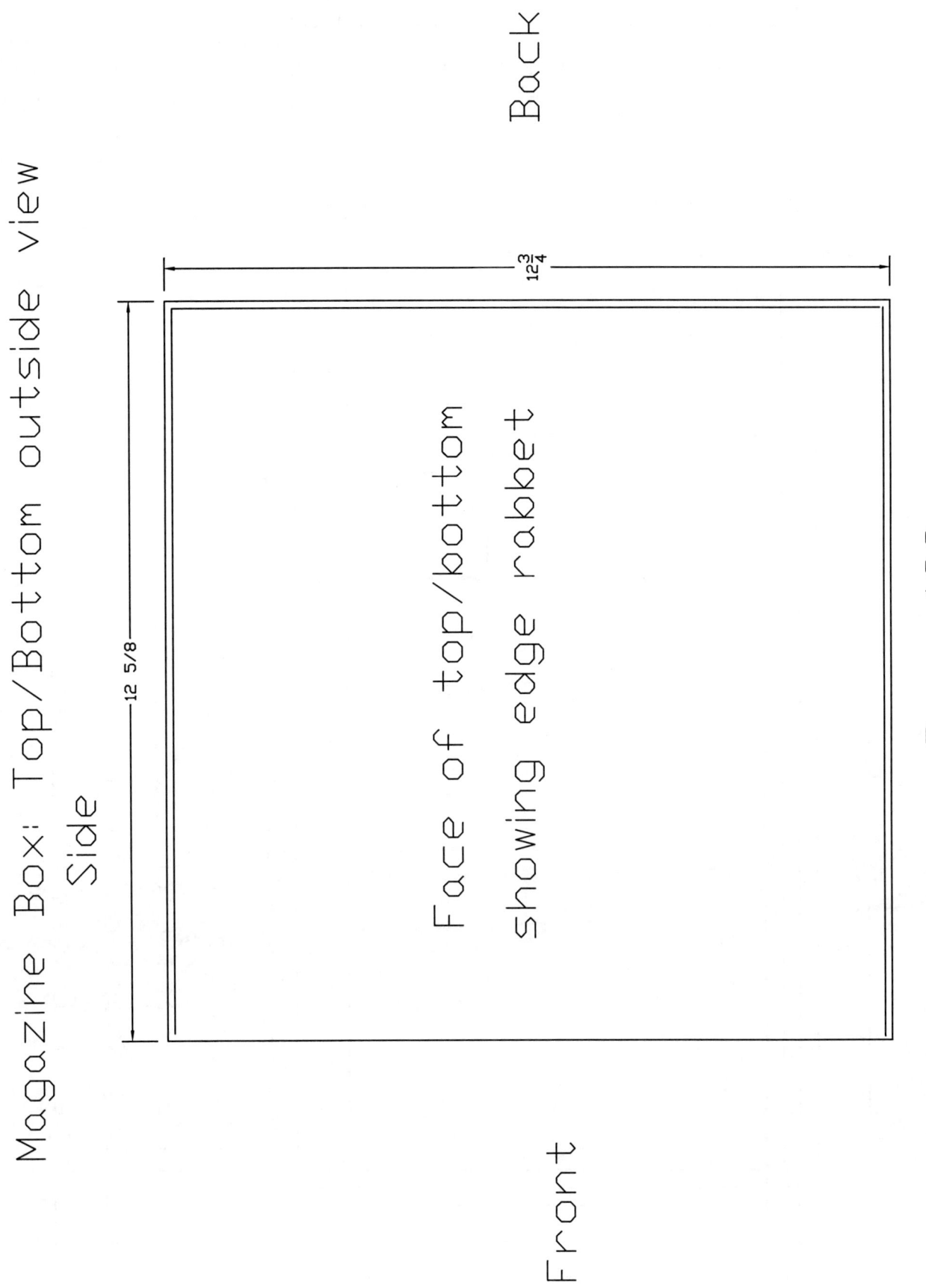

Side

12 5/8

12 3/4

Face of top/bottom showing edge rabbet

Front

Back

Page 133

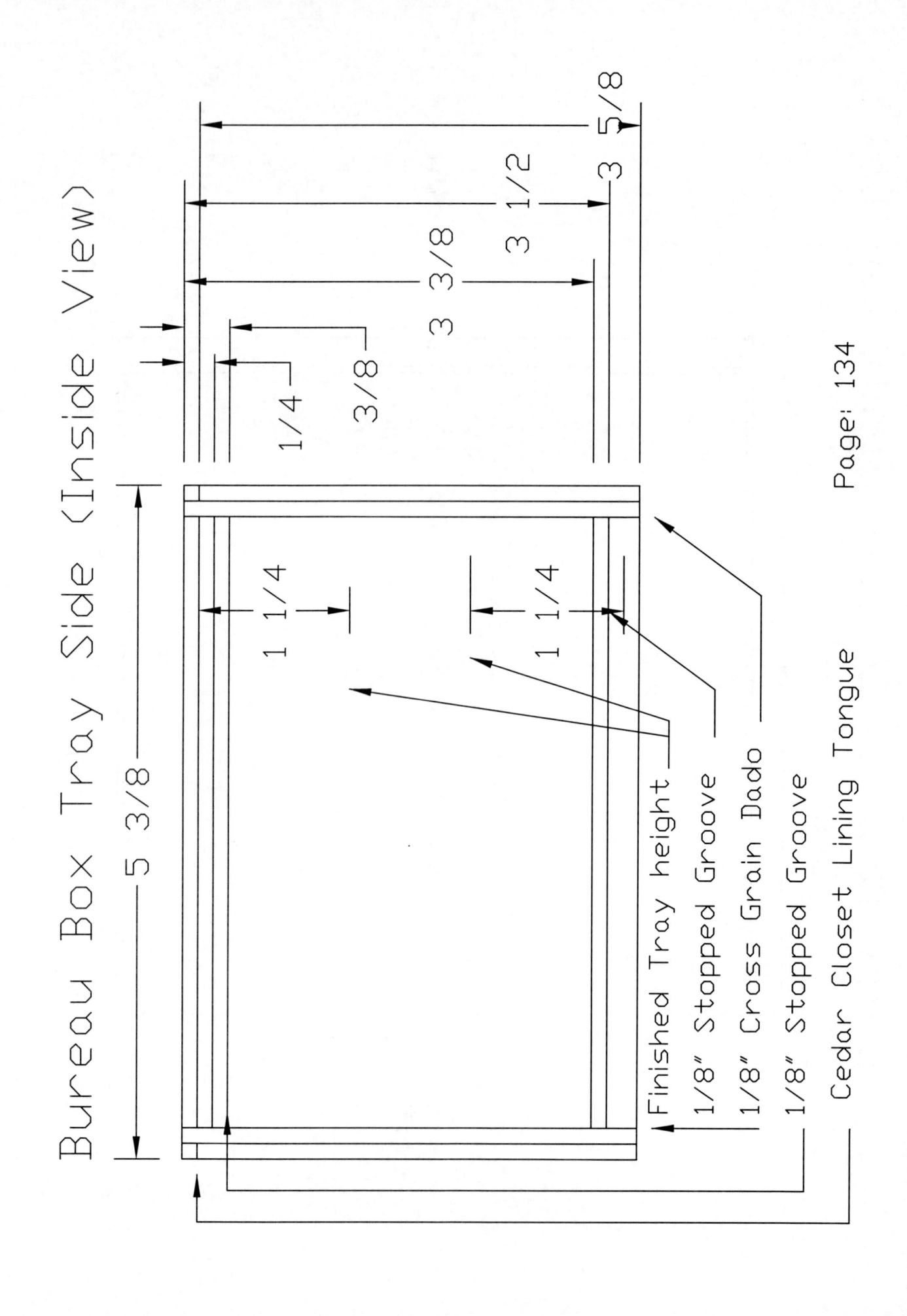

Bureau Box Tray Side (Inside View)

Dimensions:
- 5 3/8 (overall height)
- 3 5/8
- 3 1/2
- 3 3/8
- 3
- 3/8
- 1/4
- 1 1/4
- 1 1/4

Labels:
- Finished Tray height
- 1/8" Stopped Groove
- 1/8" Cross Grain Dado
- 1/8" Stopped Groove
- Cedar Closet Lining Tongue

Page: 134

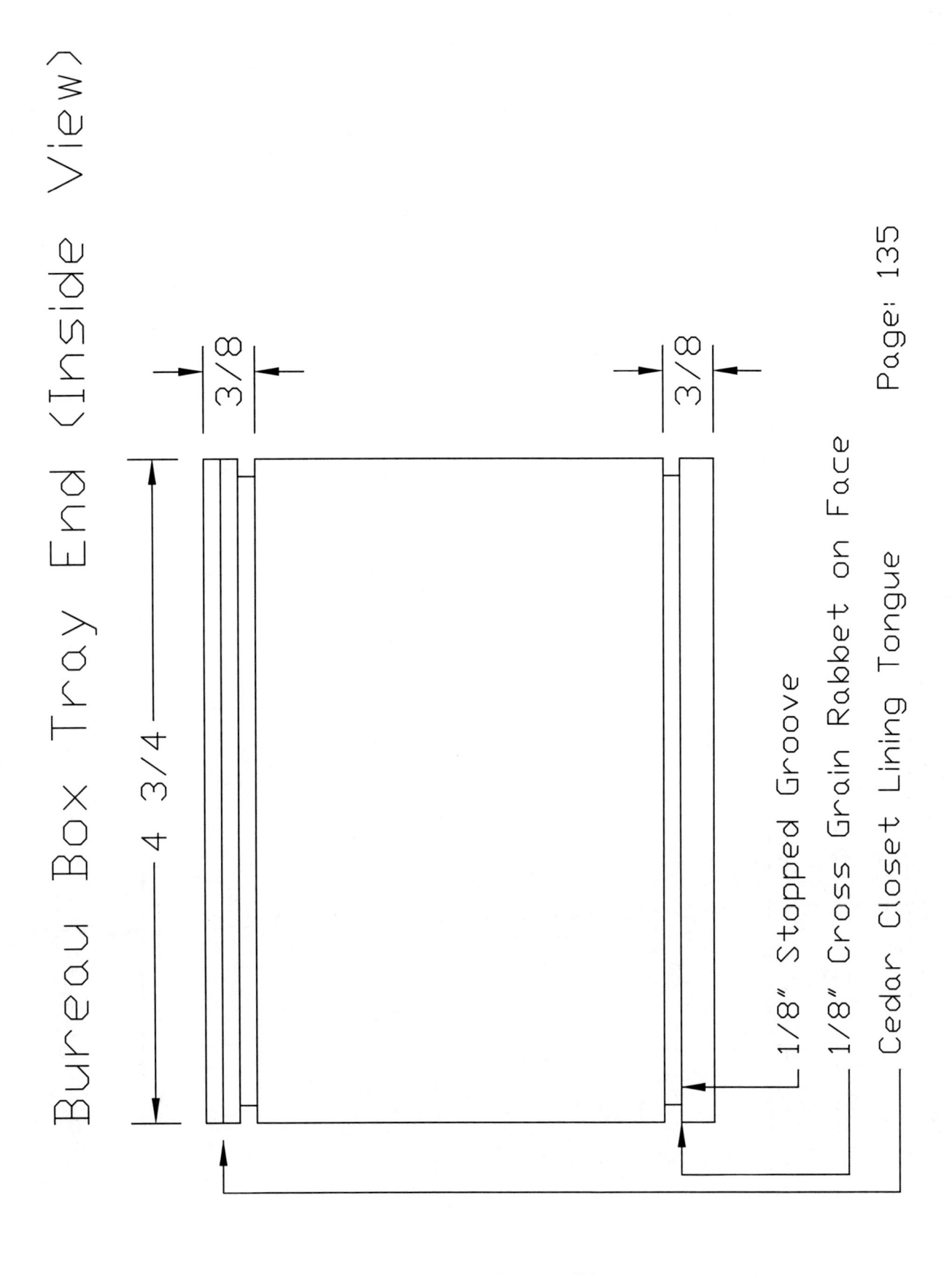

Bureau Box Tray End (Inside View)

- 3/8
- 3/8
- 4 3/4
- 1/8" Stopped Groove
- 1/8" Cross Grain Rabbet on Face
- Cedar Closet Lining Tongue

Page: 135

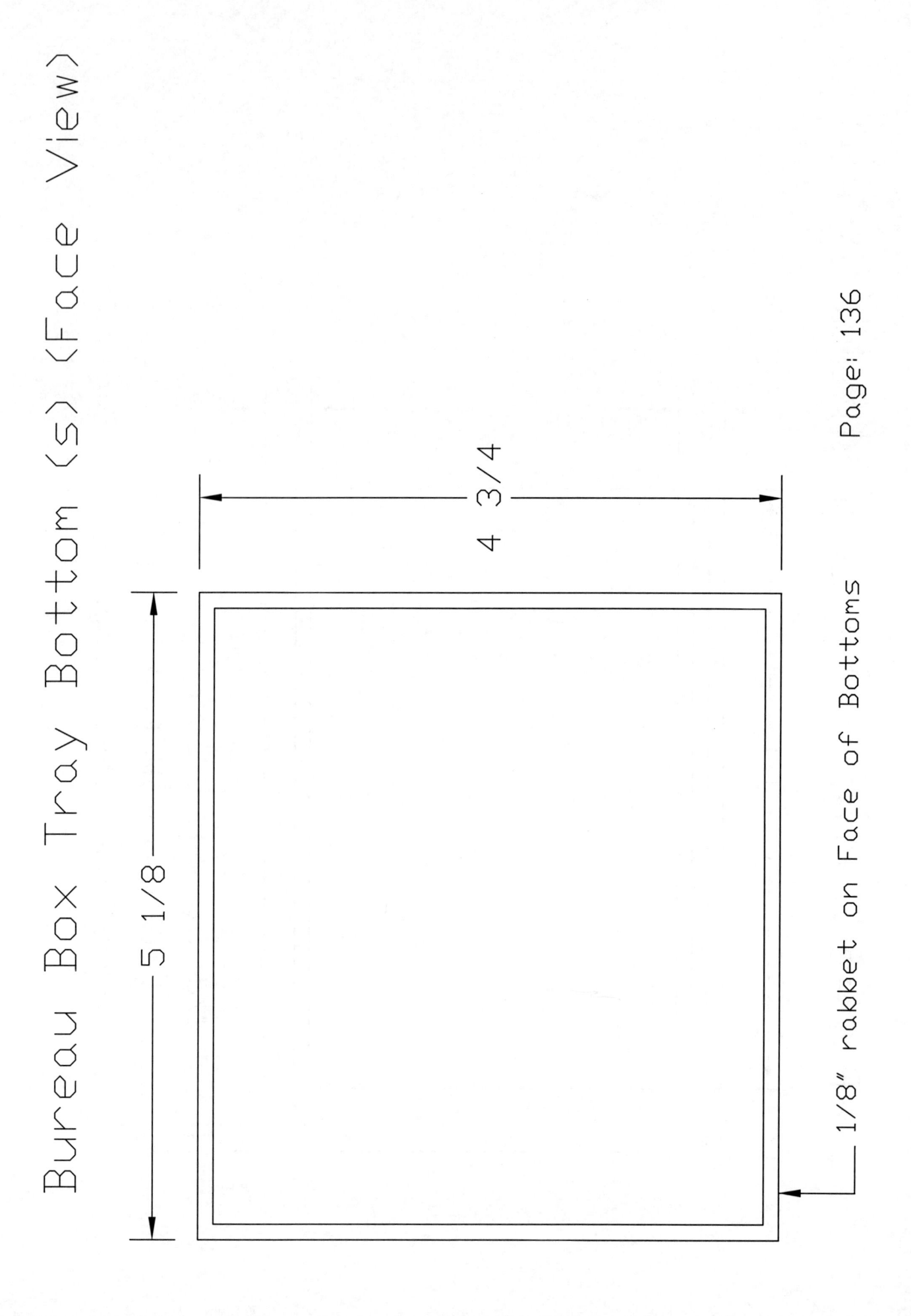

Bureau Box Tray Bottom (s) (Face View)

4 3/4

5 1/8

1/8" rabbet on Face of Bottoms

Page: 136

Bureau Box:
Side View Front Panel   Front/Back (Inside) Panels

1/4" Top Panel
1/8" Stopped groove
1/8" Case Splitting Kerf
1/4" Tray Rail
Tongue and Groove Seam
1/8" Through dado
1/8" Stopped groove
1/4" Bottom Panel

Brass Nails (#18 x 1/2) --3 per rail

11 3/4"

7/8"
3/4"
1 1/8"
3 3/4"
6 1/8"

Page: 137

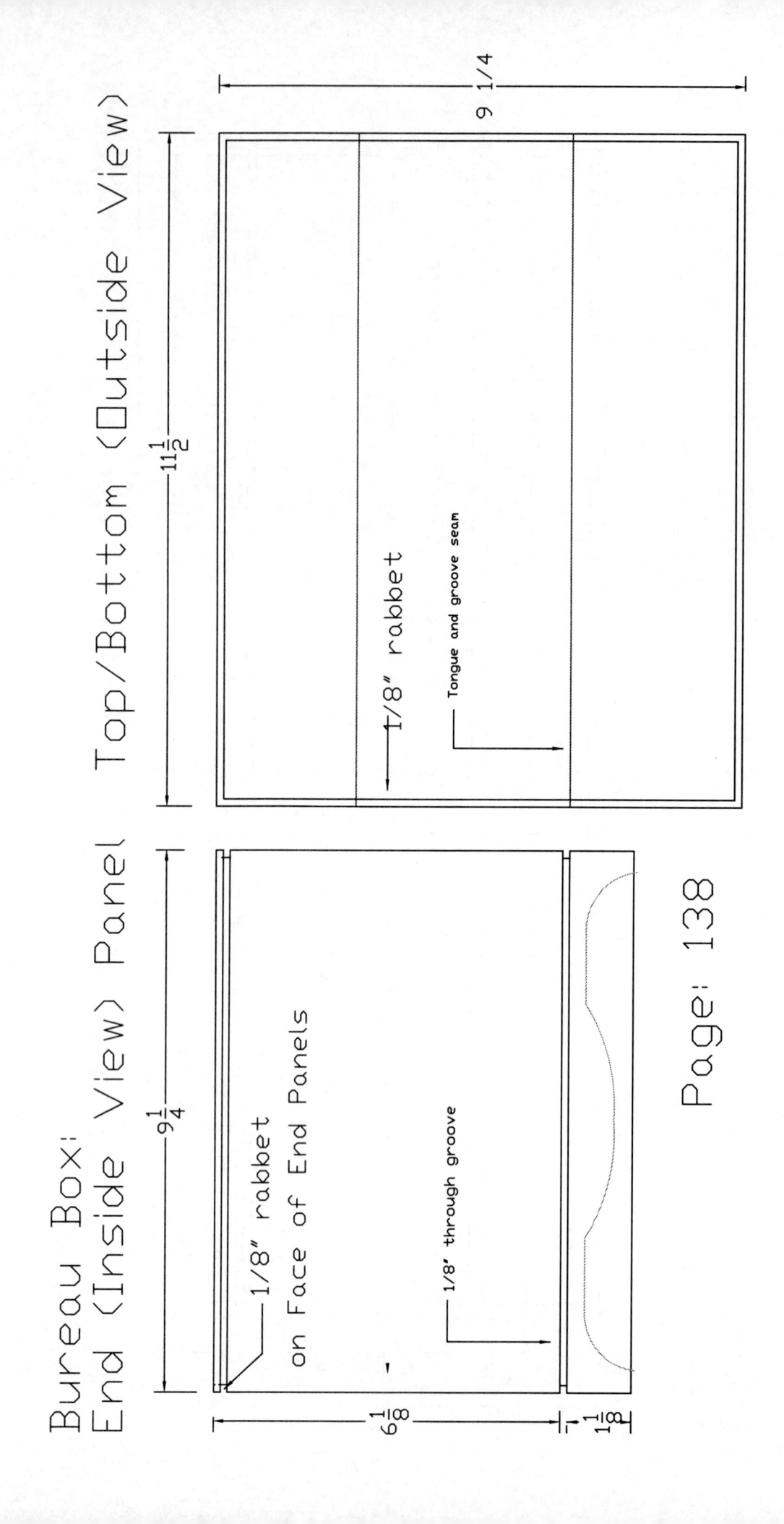

Bureau Box: End (Inside View) Panel

Top/Bottom (Outside View)

9 1/4
9
11 1/2

1/8" rabbet

Tongue and groove seam

9 1/4
6 1/8
1 1/8

1/8" rabbet on Face of End Panels

1/8" through groove

Page: 138

Bureau Box: Accessories
Sash Chain Lid Retainer

$\frac{3}{4}$

3/16

Saw kerf

$1\frac{1}{2}$

$\frac{3}{8}$

$\frac{3}{4}$

$\frac{3}{8}$

Page: 139

Bureau Box: Accessories
Clasp; Back & Side View

1/4" Dowel

Washer

#2-3/8 R. H. Screw

3 3/8

1/2
2 1/8
3/4

3 1/8
1 3/8
1 3/8

Page: 140

Shelf Profile

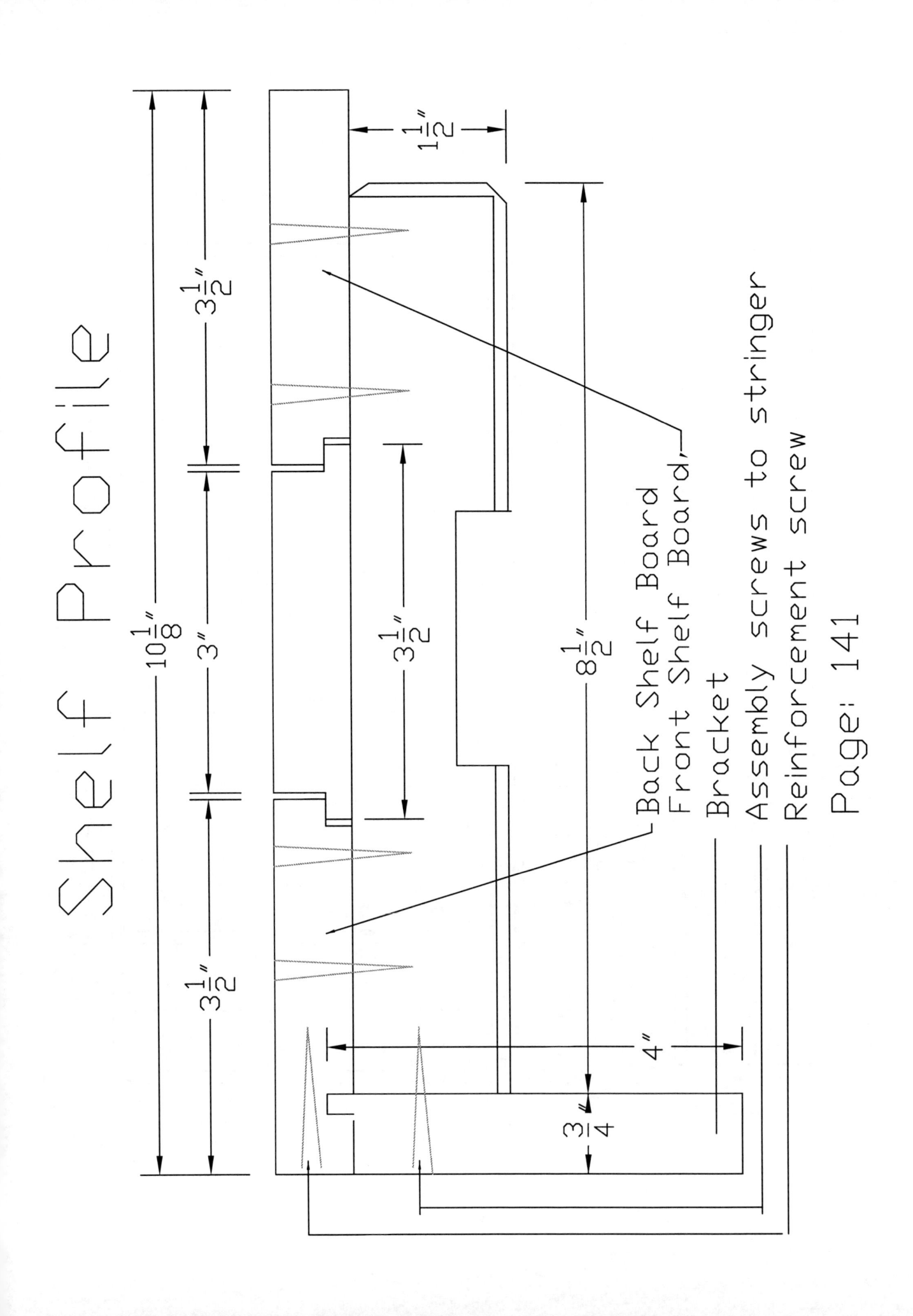

- Back Shelf Board
- Front Shelf Board
- Bracket
- Assembly screws to stringer
- Reinforcement screw

Page: 141

Stringer

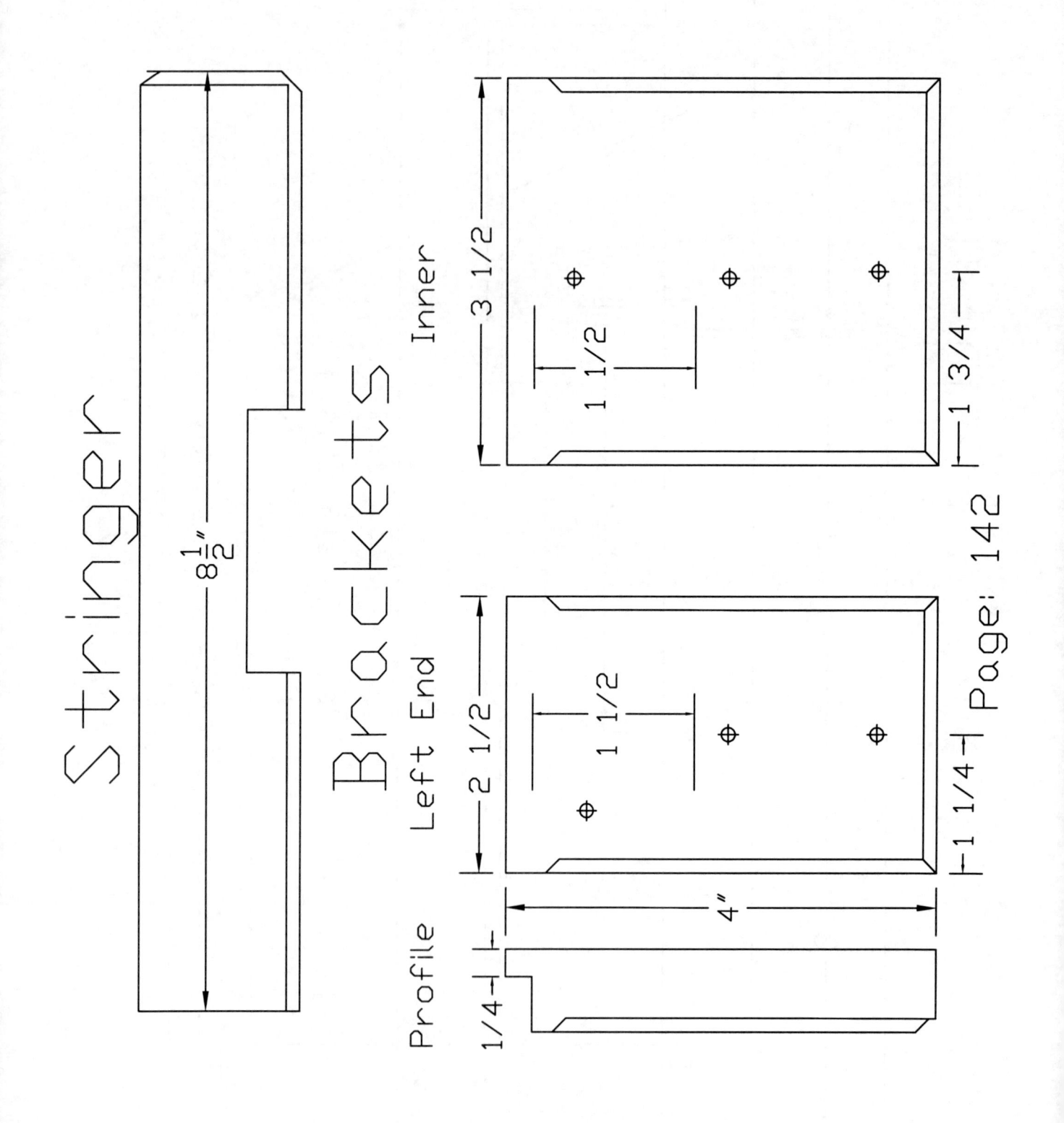

8 1/2"

Brackets

Inner

3 1/2
1 1/2
1 3/4

Left End

2 1/2
1 1/2
1 1/4

Profile

4"
1/4

Page: 142

Stringer Template
1 x 2 Fence

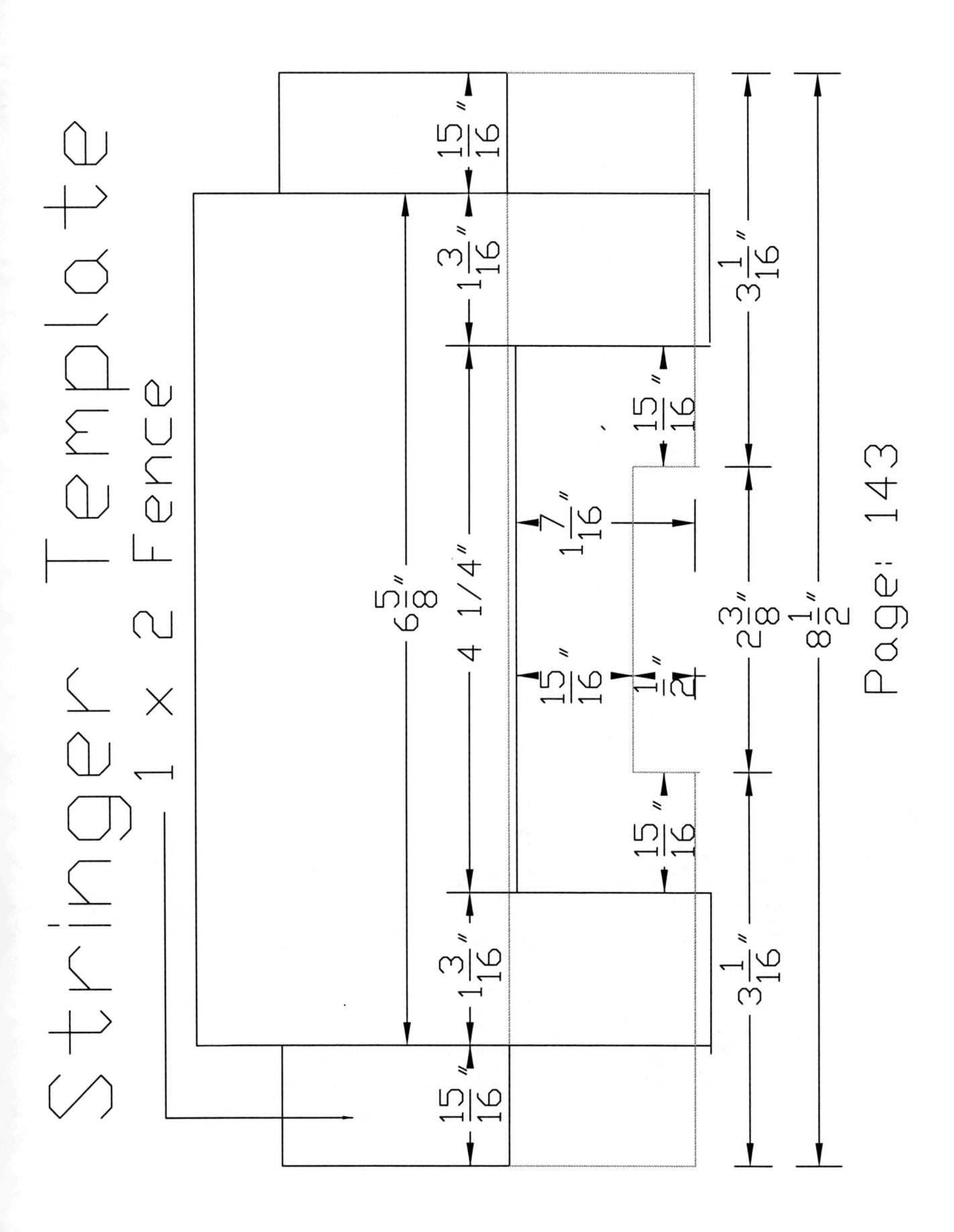

Computer Table Cutting Diagram from 4 x 8 Sheet

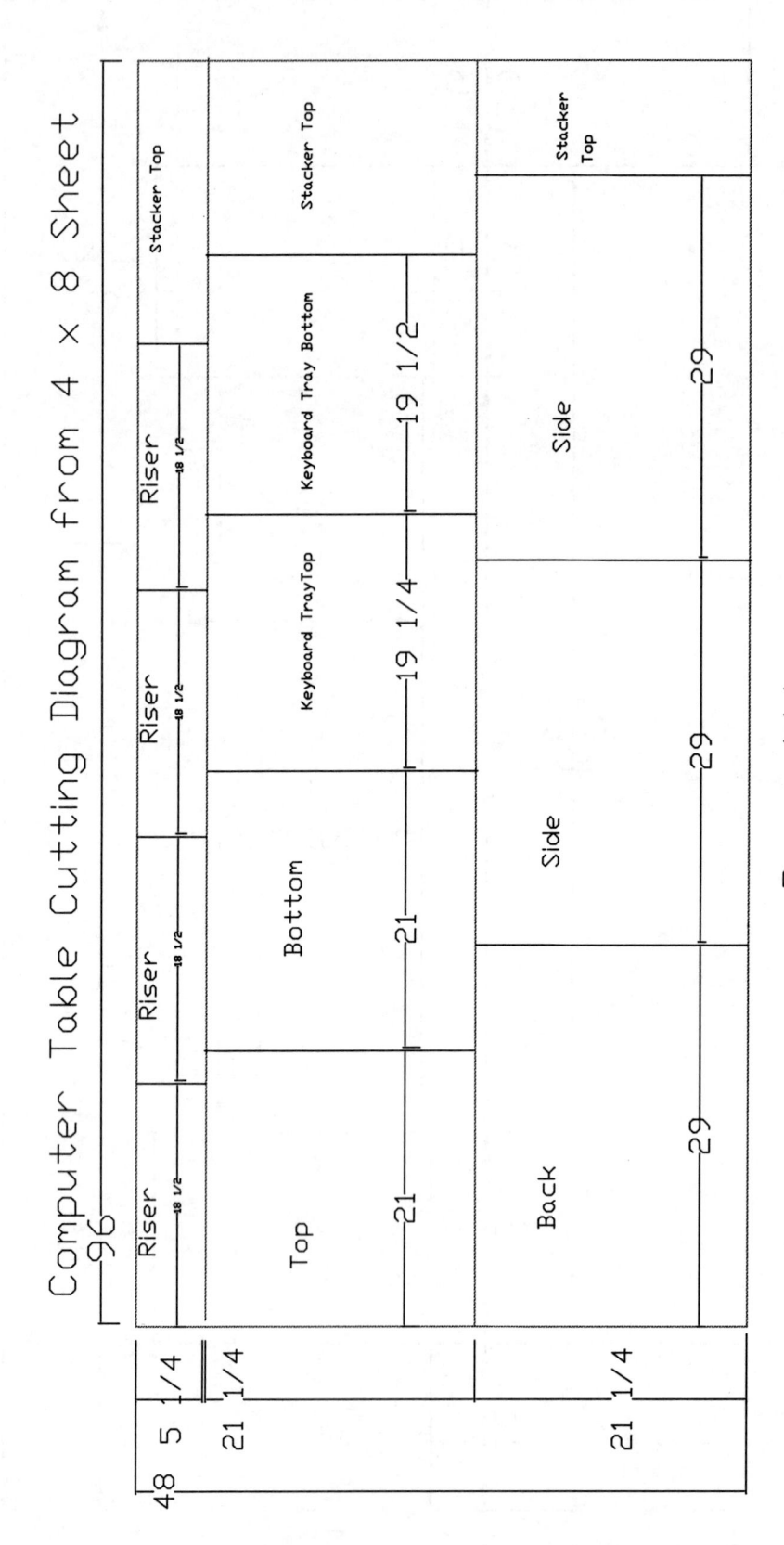

Template for hand holds

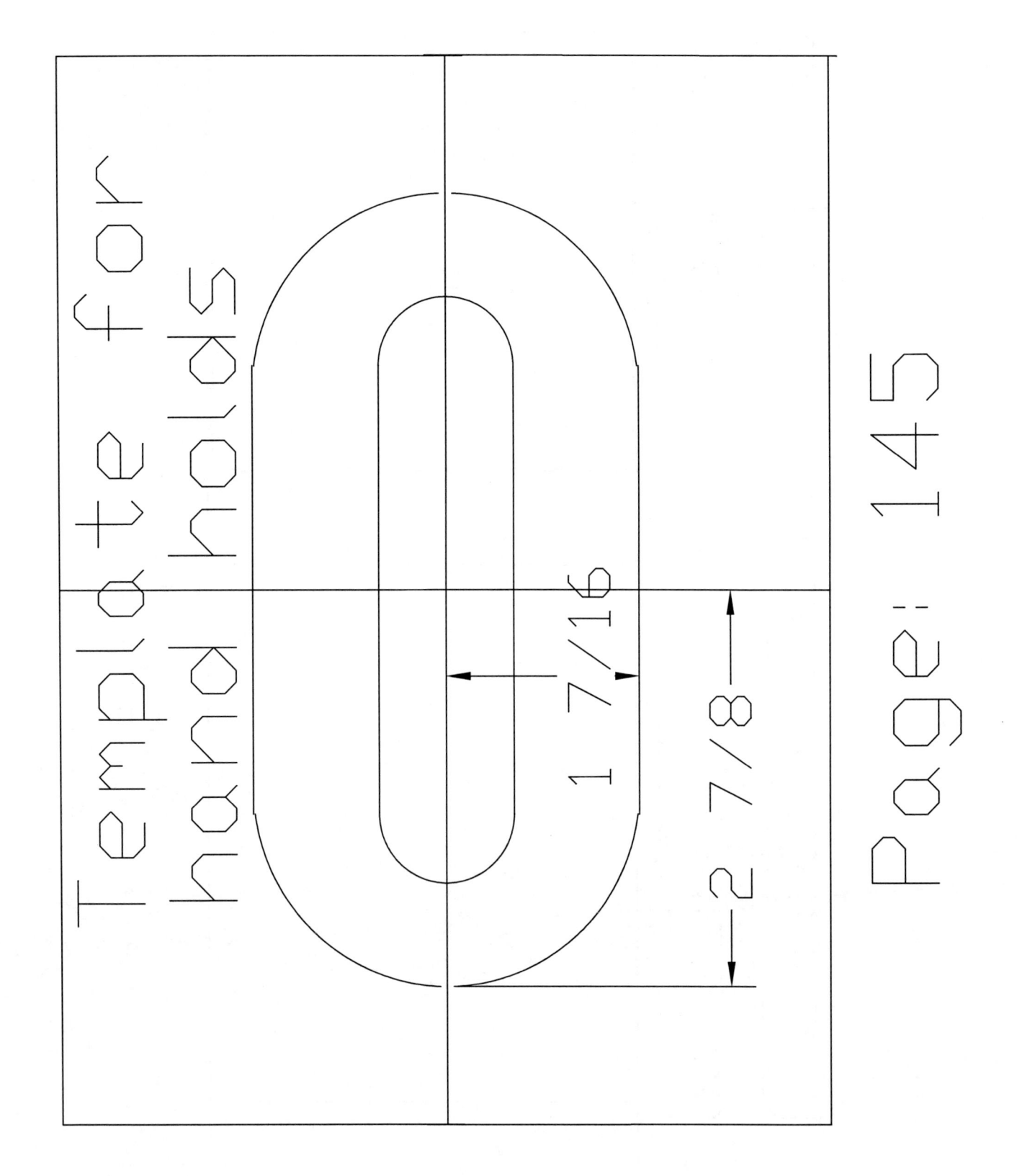

1 7/16

2 7/8

Page: 145

Computer Table

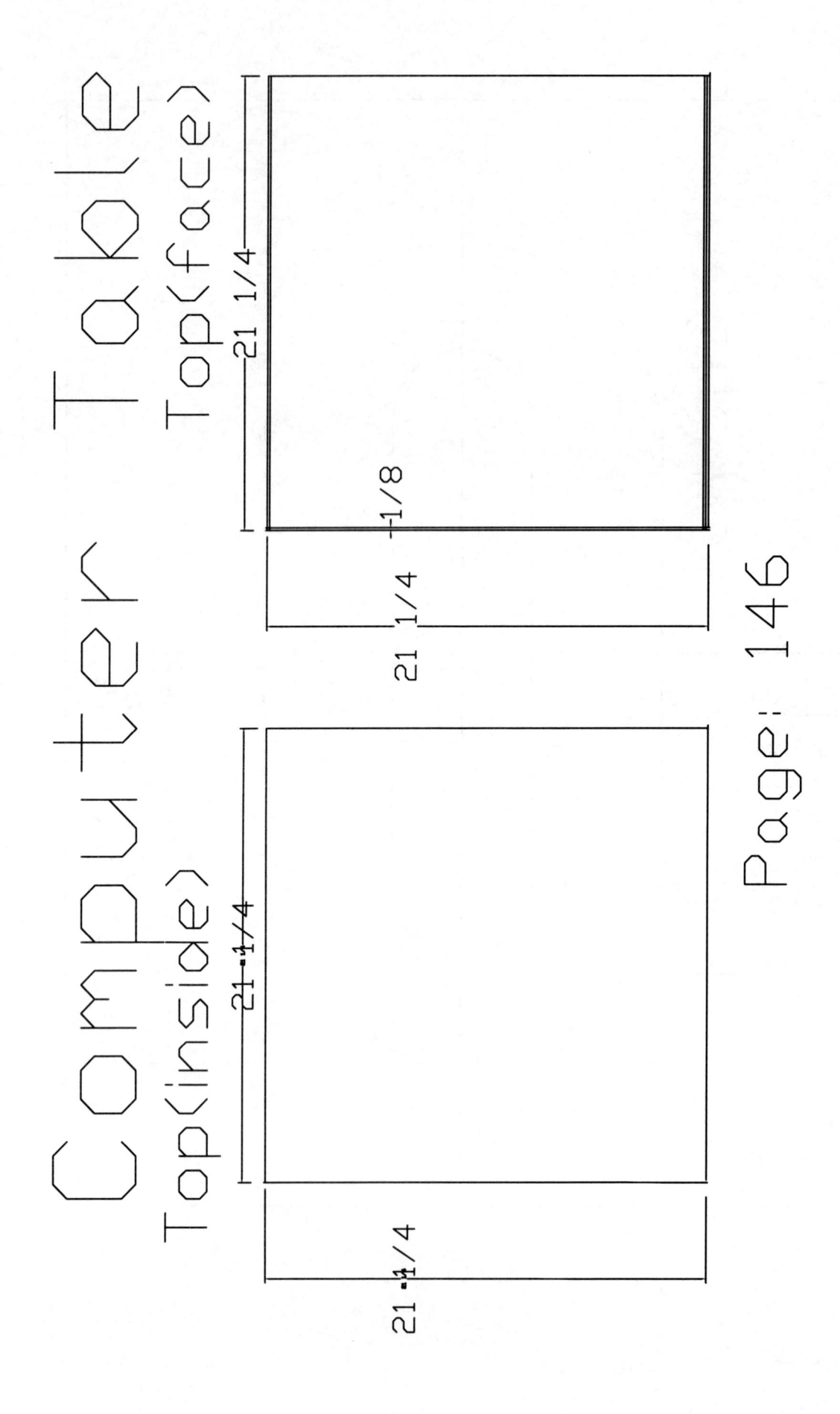

Top(inside)

21-1/4

21-1/4

Top(face)

21 1/4

21 1/4

1/8

Page: 146

Back(face)

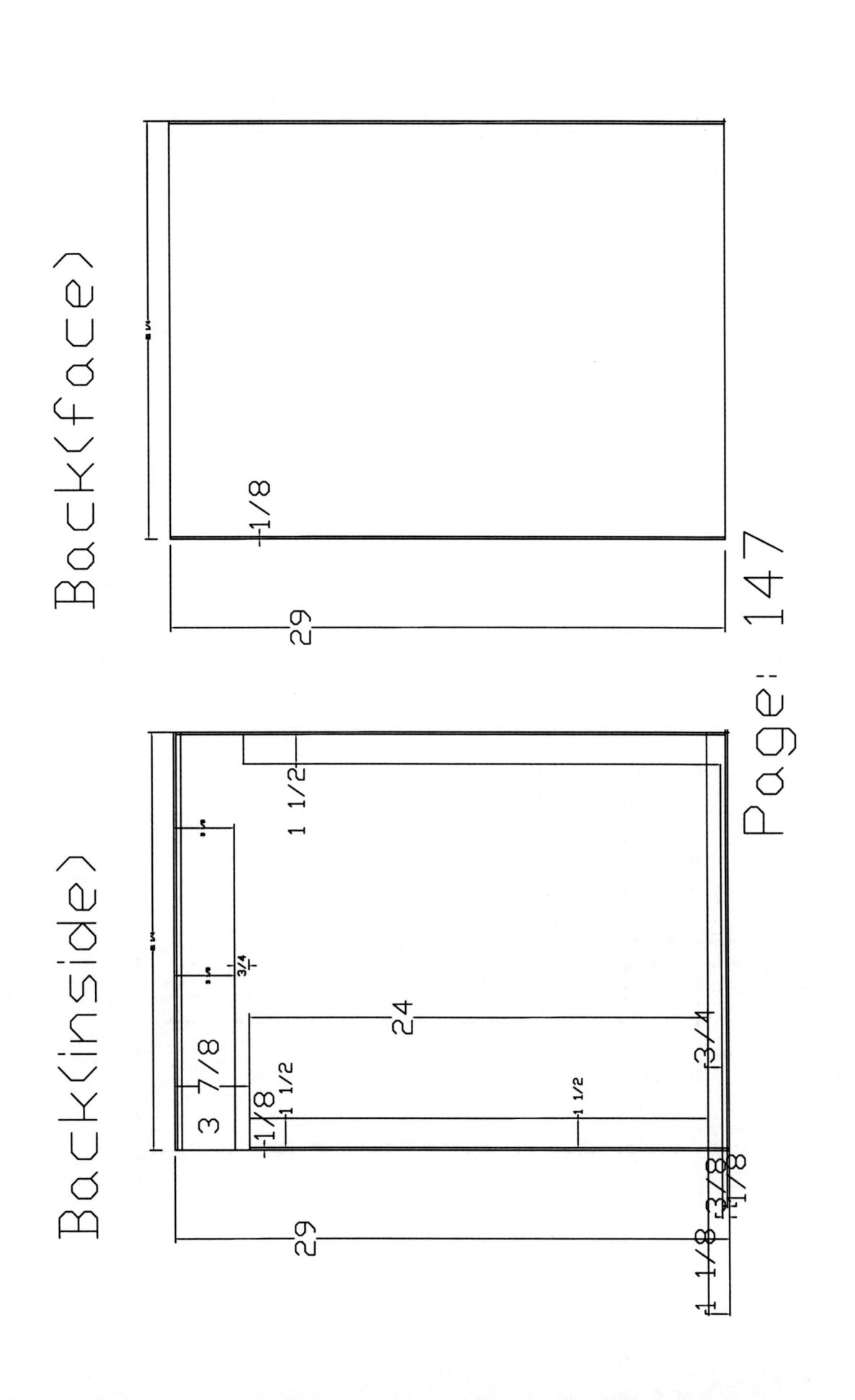

Back(inside)

Page: 147

Side(face)

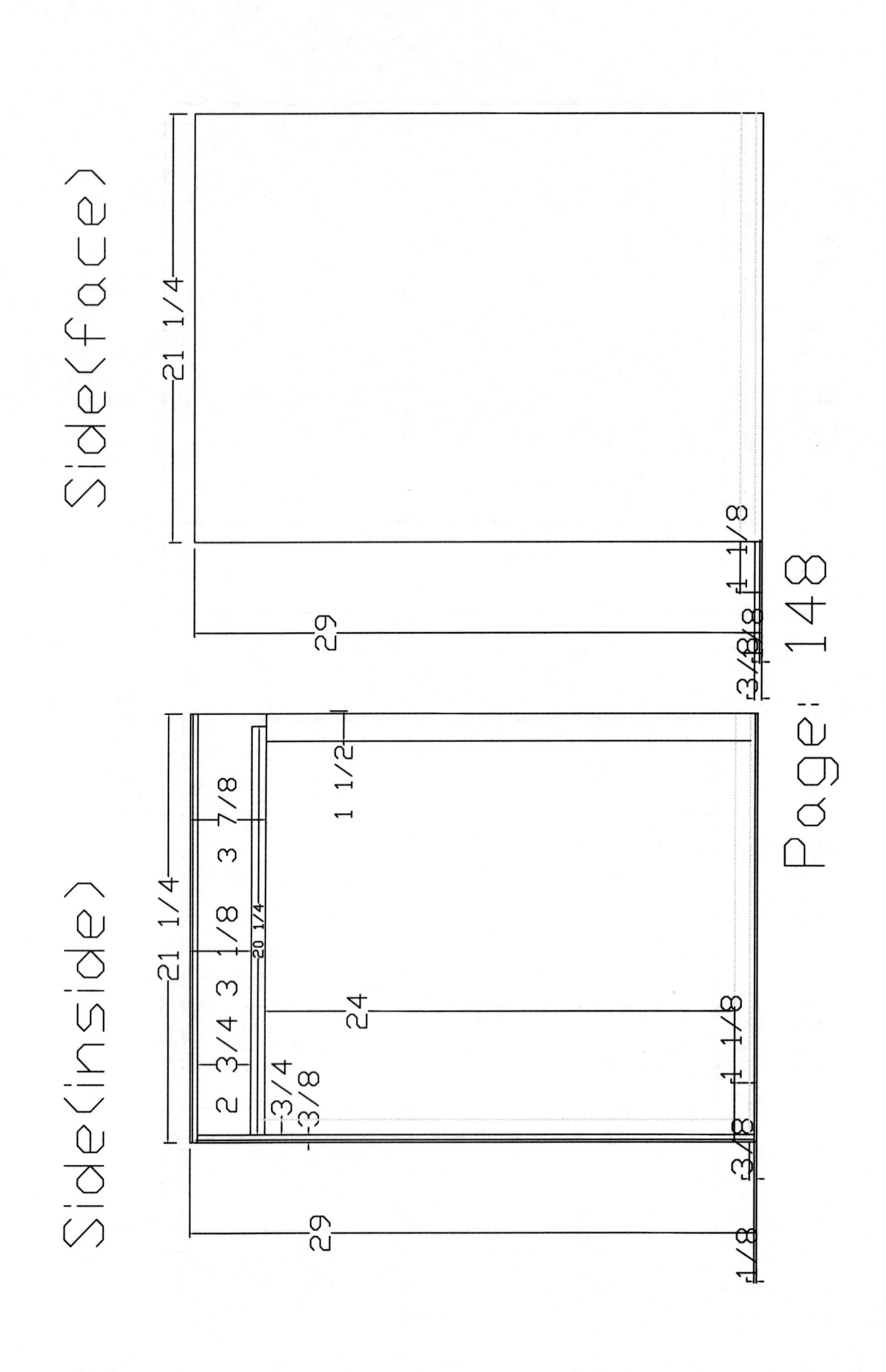

21 1/4

29

3/8 1 1/8

Side(inside)

21 1/4

2 3/4 3 1/8 3 7/8

3/4
3/8

20 1/4

1 1/2

24

1 1/8

29

3/8

1/8

Page: 148

Bottom(face)

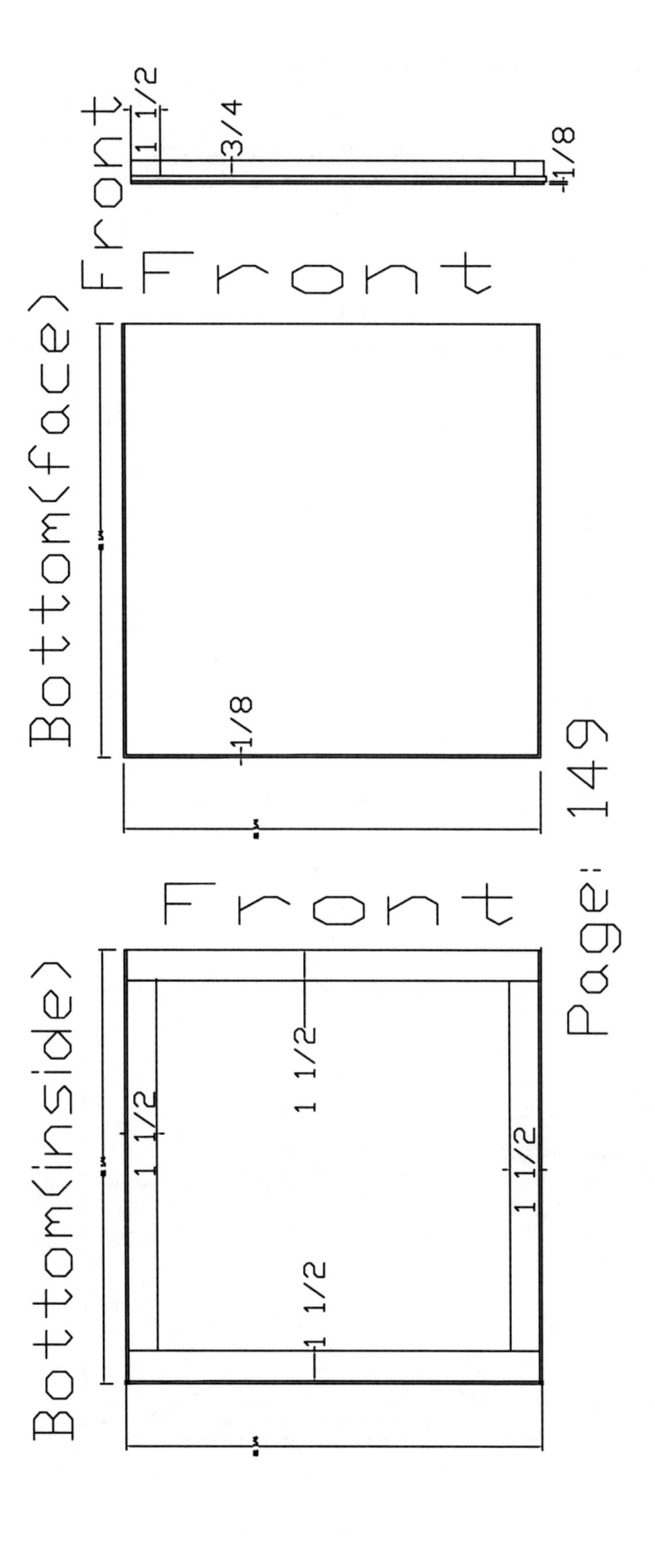

Front

1 1/2
3/4
1/8

1/8

Bottom(inside)

Front

1 1/2
1 1/2
1 1/2
1 1/2

Page: 149

Tray: Top w/front   Bottom   Profile

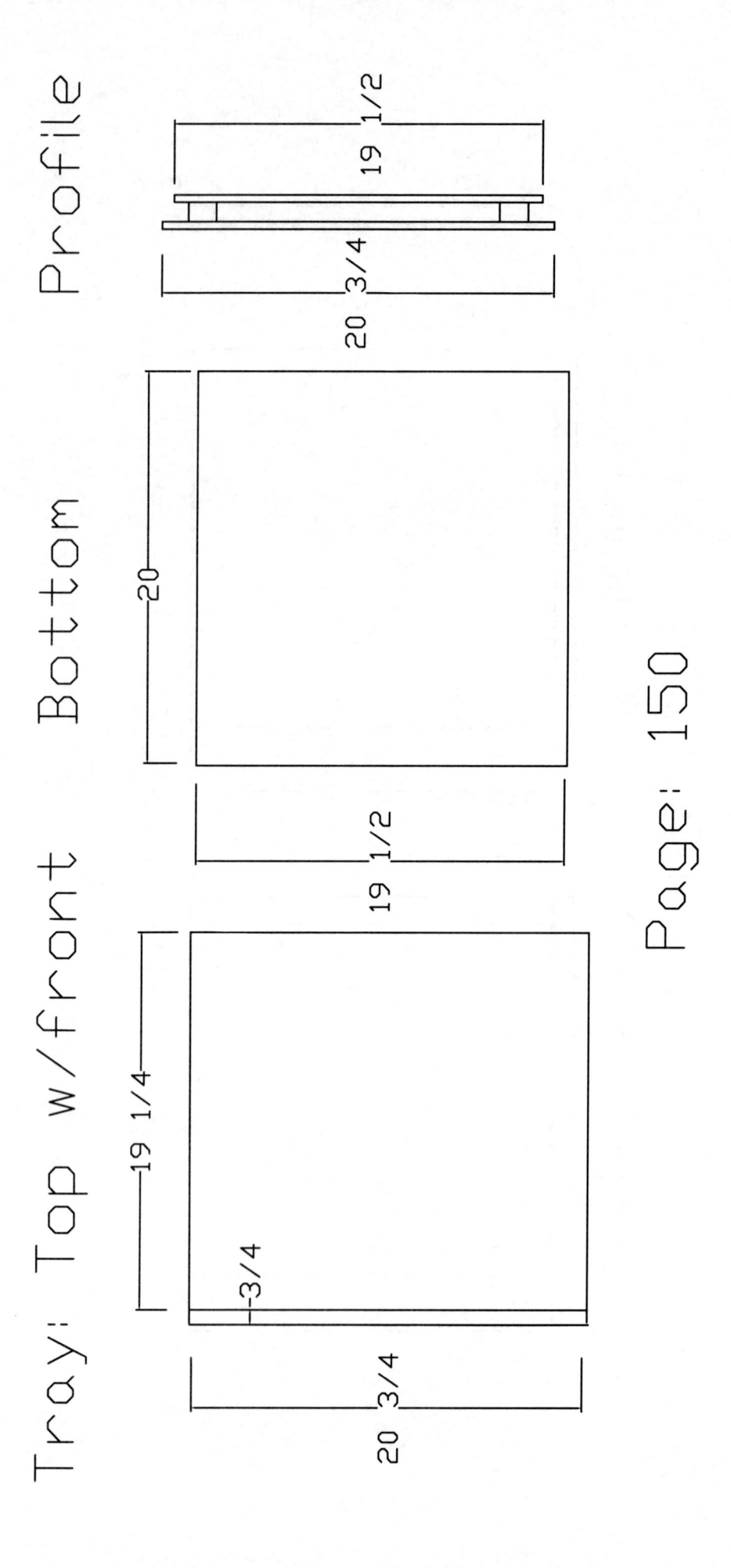

Top w/front: 20 3/4 × 19 1/4 (with 3/4 front strip)

Bottom: 20 × 19 1/2

Profile: 20 3/4 / 19 1/2

Page: 150

Large Stacker

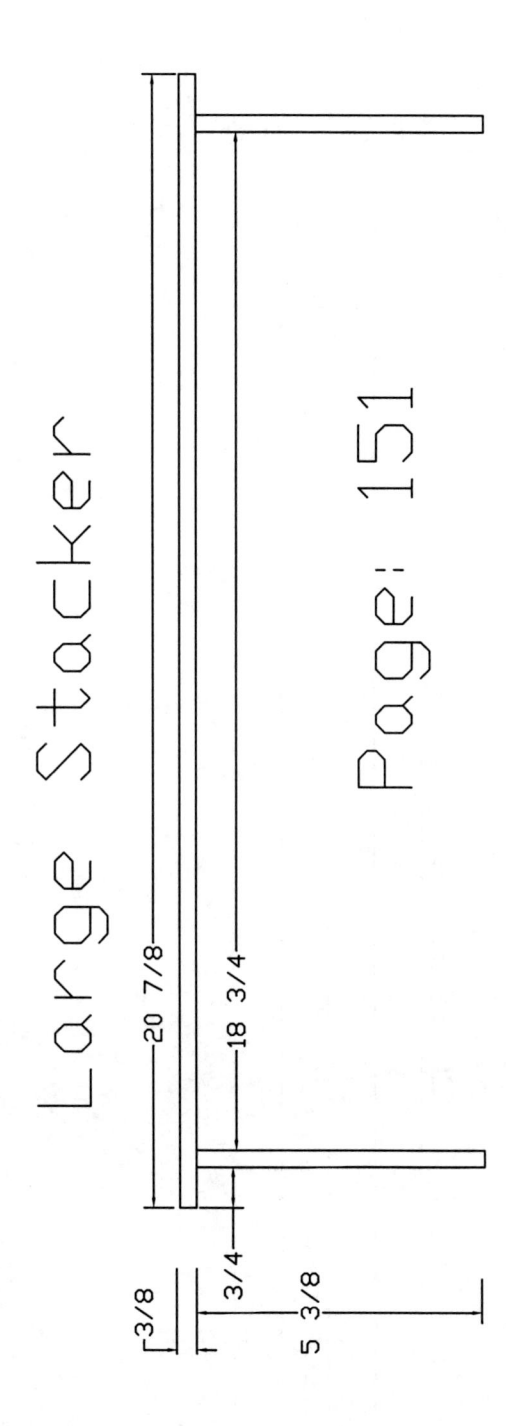

Page: 151

20 7/8
18 3/4
3/8
3/4
5 3/8

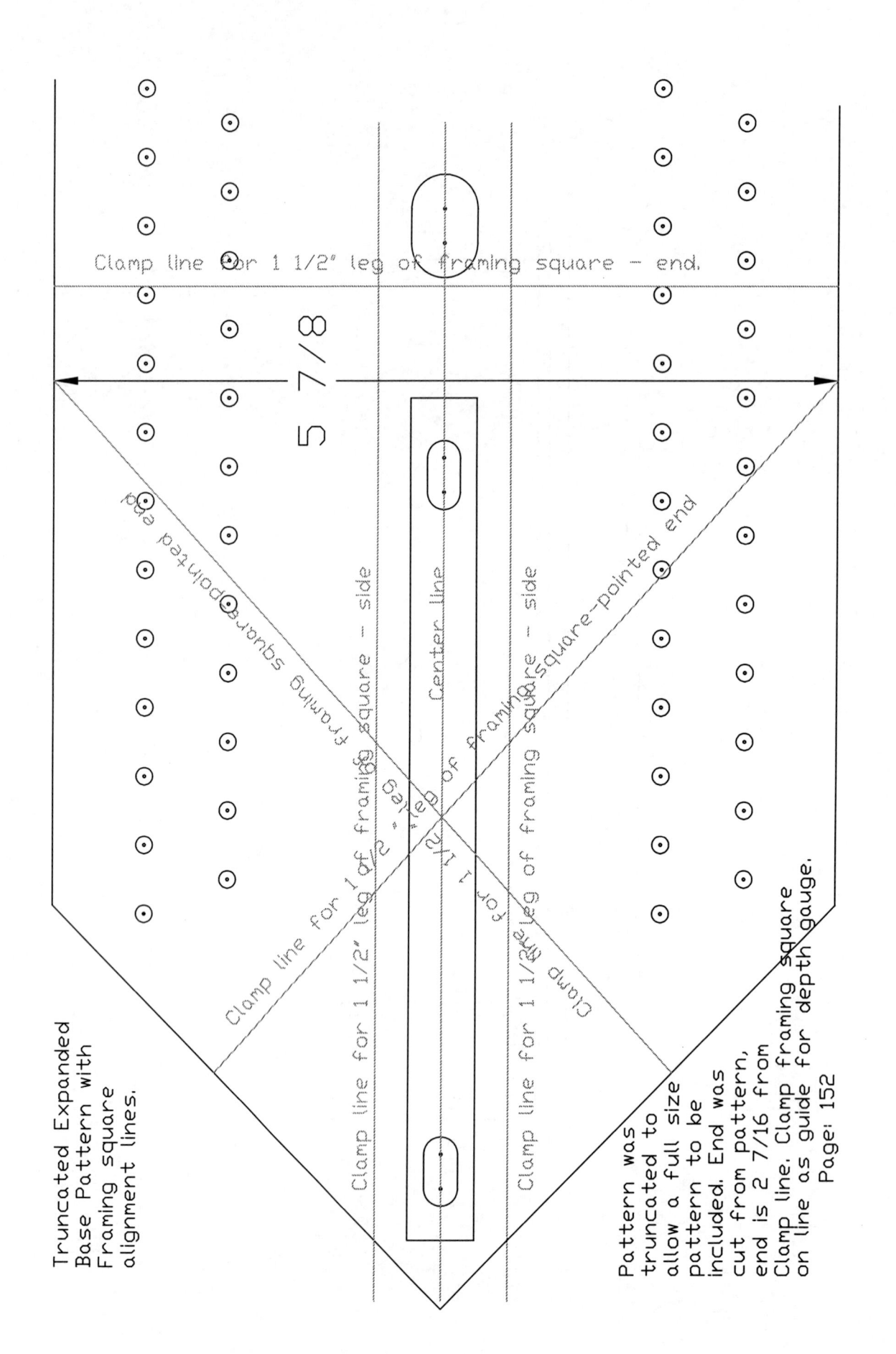

Truncated Expanded Base Pattern with Framing square alignment lines.

Clamp line for 1 1/2" leg of framing square – end.

5 7/8

Clamp line for 1 1/2" leg of framing square – side

Center line

Clamp line for 1 1/2" leg of framing square-pointed end

Clamp line for 1 1/2" leg of framing square – side

Clamp line for 1 1/2" leg of framing square-pointed end

Pattern was truncated to allow a full size pattern to be included. End was cut from pattern, end is 2 7/16 from Clamp line. Clamp framing square on line as guide for depth gauge.

Page: 152

WorkBench: Side view, Top View

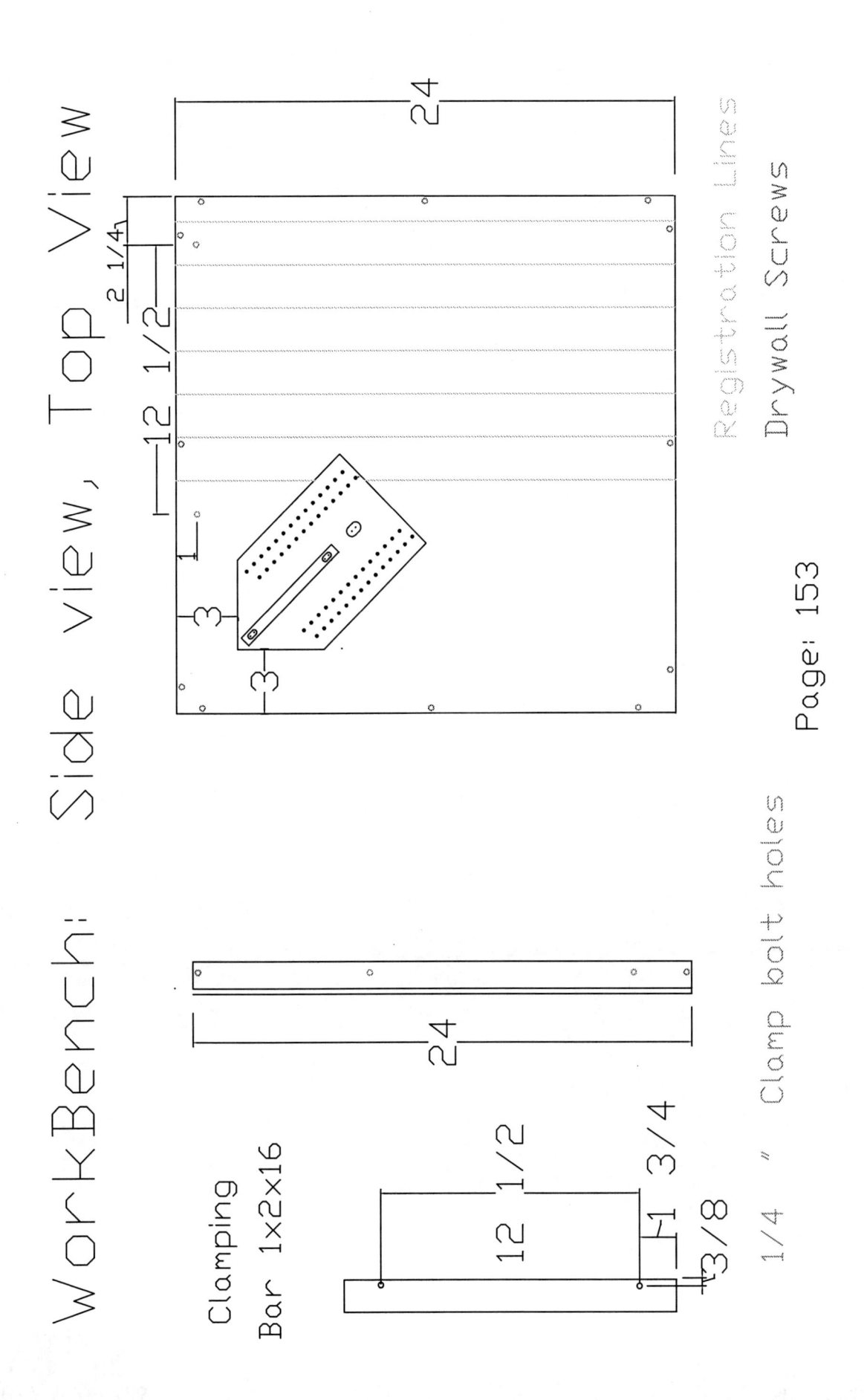

Clamping
Bar 1x2x16

Registration Lines
Drywall Screws

1/4" Clamp bolt holes

Page: 153